Freedom from Anger

Complete list of Christian books by Gary Schulz

The Greatest Command
Hope for the Depressed
Become a Biblical Marriage Counselor
May They Be One
Relationships —Why Jesus Came
From God's Perspective
From Victim to Victory
The Discipling Father
Setting the Captives Free
New Wine New Wineskins
God's Creation of the Sexual Union
If You Love Me...
Partners
Saved from our Enemies
Good News of Jesus Christ
Eternal Life What Is It?
God's Creation of Work
The Power Of God's Grace
God's Creation, The Family
Marriage Enrichment
Passing Your Faith
Freedom From Anger
Clearly Seen
Creation to Rebellion to Restoration
Oil In Your Lamp
Wimps!
Controlling Parent Controlling Child
Restoring Broken Walls

www.kingdomcomepublications.com

Freedom from Anger
A Biblical Study

[Christian Anger Management]
[(CAM]

Gary Schulz

Kingdom Come Publications
81 Oaklawn Dr.
Midland, MI 48640

www.kingdomcomepublications.com

Printed in the United State of America

Contents

Preface

Anger is becoming an epidemic in our society. Child abuse is so prevalent that we cannot spank our children in public anymore for fear that someone will turn us in. Our prisons and jails are filled with people who are there because of violent crimes. We can't even drive down the highway without fear that someone will cut us off out of road-rage. Verbal anger is a constant threat. Our angry words ruin more relationships than most any other offense. These emotional words ruin friendships, employment, marriages, divide neighbors, relatives, brothers and sisters, children and parents. There is no end to the destruction caused by anger.

This class began as an adult Sunday school study. The biblical study and the open sharing revealed a deep hidden need. People that I saw every week were opening up with deep, serious problems that aroused their anger. They wanted freedom, but for years they had remained captives.

It soon followed that God opened an opportunity to teach this class in prison. *Freedom from Anger* began as a pilot class in the Saginaw Correctional Facility in Freeland, Michigan. The course was readily accepted as a routine offering due to the effectiveness of this heart felt study. It has become a four month course that is offered several times per year to several levels of prisoners. It is taught entirely by volunteers, and over the years we have seen God work powerfully to bring freedom to men who have been captive to their angry behavior.

Many people outside of the prison requested that we offer this class because they knew they were experiencing the same bondage and destruction caused by anger. Everyone struggles with anger at some level.

This class has been proven to benefit those with mild or occasional anger problems to those with very deep rooted and even abusive anger issues. It has been taught in and out of the prison, and it is highly recommended that both husband and wife attend, even if only one spouse is seen as having the "serious" anger problem. We have seen serious marriage problems resolved as a consequence of this teaching. We have seen people take on a totally different attitude about their work and workplace. They have replaced agony with joy. We have seen many relationships restored. We have seen many offensive behaviors transformed into pleasant relationships. We have seen many draw close to God. We have seen many come to salvation through Jesus Christ.

This book can serve as an individual study, but its main purpose is to facilitate instructors and small group leaders as they develop classes in their communities. There is no substitute for the many personal interactions that occur in a class. Typically, a lesson is taught in one or two ninety minute sessions. The Instructor will teach the lesson in about half the time in an informal session with welcomed participation from the students. This is followed by sharing in small groups of three to six. Each person answers specific questions that are provided for each lesson, and can be found at the end of each chapter of this book.

Many scripture references are given throughout. Some are printed and some you will have to look up from the reference. Keep a Bible with you as you study.

Jesus said, "For where two or three come together in my name, there am I with them." Matthew 18:20 This has been most certainly true in the class sessions as we heard from the Lord as each person spoke among us. We saw things we might never have seen alone. This book is no substitute for the class, but it is my prayer that through your reading that you will see things about God and yourself that will set you free.

Chapter One

Anger Can Be a Repetitive Trap

Where does anger come from? Like many of our emotions, anger is part of our created spiritual being. But most of us struggle with our anger. At times it is appropriate. Jesus was angry with the money changers in the temple. He turned over their tables and chased them out with a whip. (John 2:15) Yet we know that Jesus did not sin, even in his actions. Anger in itself, as an emotion, is not necessarily sin. Paul quoted Psalm 4:4, "In your anger, do not sin." Ephesians 4:26. However, most of us struggle with our anger in that we do sin. We may sin in our actions toward another, or privately in our hearts.

Where does all this sinful anger come from? Well, our sinful nature. But just as we inherited our sinful nature, we can inherit many of the driving forces of our anger.

ANGER PASSED FROM GENERATION TO GENERATION

Most of the time, serious anger is passed from generation to generation. For example, an angry father treats his own children with anger. He may physically abuse them. He may yell at them. He may verbally abuse them

1

with degrading words. He may <u>abuse their mother</u>. He may even abuse them by <u>abandonment</u>. Abandonment may come with complete absence, but it could also be by too many hours at work or <u>selfish preoccupation</u>, such as television or sports.

The point is that angry parents will treat their children in a harmful way because of their anger, and this will harm the heart of their children such that when they grow up, they may become angry parents. And so the cycle continues—anger gets passed on from parent to child, parent to child, generation after generation.

The anger from childhood creates a wound in the heart that can fester for years—maybe an entire lifetime. A man or woman who has a wounded heart from childhood can carry that wound and the anger that proceeds from it into old age, even after their parents have been dead and gone for decades. The wound and the cause of the wound are hidden from most of us. But the anger and angry behavior are not at all hidden. They can plague our lives like an incurable disease that destroys our relationships all around us and robs us of the joy of life.

The family is responsible for much that is passed on from generation to generation. Anger is just one aspect. What gets passed on can be good or bad; depending upon what behavior is present.

Let's look at two real people and their offspring. A popular analysis of Max Jukes and Jonathan Edwards, who lived in the 1800's, gives a good comparative example of the reality of family influence:

"Max Jukes, the atheist, lived a godless life. He married an ungodly girl, and from the union there were 310 who died as paupers, 150 were criminals, 7 were murderers, 100 were drunkards, and more than half of the women were prostitutes. His 540 descendants cost the State one and a quarter million dollars."

"But, praise the Lord, it works both ways! There is a record of a great American man of God, Jonathan Edwards. He lived at the same time as Max Jukes, but he married a godly girl. An investigation was made of 1,394 known descendants of Jonathan Edwards of which 13 became college presidents, 65 college professors, 3 United States senators, 30 judges, 100 lawyers, 60 physicians, 75 army and navy officers, 100 preachers and missionaries, 60 authors of prominence, one a vice-president of the United States, 80 became public officials in other capacities, 295 college graduates, among whom were governors of states and ministers to foreign countries. His descendants did not cost the state a single penny."

It should be obvious that what we pass on to our children can progress on to many generations. The consequences of our wounded hearts can be in the form of addictive behaviors. Addictions can be mistaken as exclusively passed on through genetics, when in fact wounds to the heart and soul by the one(s) who should have loved us the most have generated the major influence. The behaviors can be passed on from generation to generation, not by the genes; rather, by the wounds. Genetics may also play a part. Some are more predisposed to medicate their problems with alcohol, drugs, food, etc. However, treating an addiction as purely biological will likely overlook some very significant spiritual roots.

I have known many alcoholics over the years, and I have also noticed that many were also struggling inside. The struggle may be a in the form of bitterness, depression, anxiety, frustration, etc., and as a consequence, anger may flare up. Somewhere along life's path they became wounded in their inner soul. These wounds can fester for a lifetime if not dealt with.

I knew a man in my workplace that was to me very calm and gentle. We were eating lunch together one day as we watched the TV news. An ad came on talking about how many of the elderly had the "disease of alcoholism". I spouted out, "Alcoholism is not a disease." When the ad was finished, my friend stated, "I don't know what it is, but I have it."

At this point I had stuck my foot in my mouth, so I explained myself, and I told him about how I thought that most alcoholism was primarily pasted on from wounded hearts, not our genes. To which he began to confess that he was abused as a child. Then when he was older and joined the Navy, he began to drink and frequently got drunk and very angry. When he left the Navy he carried his anger and drinking into his marriage. His behavior has had its detrimental effects on his wife and children to this day.

3

In his mid-forties he decided to commit himself to a clinic that worked on his anger, and he became free of the anger.

This conversation between us took place about a dozen years after his treatment in the clinic, for he was now in his fifties. I asked him, "Have you had a struggle with drinking since then?" And he said, "No, I am not so foolish as to frequent a bar, but I do not desire to drink."

I felt relieved that my "foot-in-the-mouth" statement had some validity in his case. I don't claim to know so much about alcoholism as to say that all of those addicted are also angry. And certainly our inherited biology may play a part. But I also know that most addictions have spiritual roots, even if there is also some biological connection to the bondage. The spiritual roots must be cut out and the wounds healed if deliverance is to be long lasting. We can walk out on our lawn and pluck off the tops of dandelions, and the lawn may look good for the moment, but tomorrow the yellow flowers will be back. The roots go deep, and the only way to be rid of them is to dig deep.

The Bible says that "wine makes life merry" (Ecclesiastes 10:19). It makes life merry because of the way we perceive life when alcohol is in our blood stream, not because our overall life has changed. Alcohol and drugs can momentarily set our hearts and minds free from the realities of life around us. They can give a temporary escape from the thoughts and feelings that torment us. Even depression is treated with drugs. Depression is a state where we are trapped in our negative, hopeless thoughts. Drugs provide an escape from this narrow focus. But drugs do not change our past, our present situation, our future, our hurts, our wounded hearts, or our understanding of life. And when the drugs stop, life goes back to its hopelessness unless there has been a spiritual intervention to the heart of the man. Jesus came for this spiritual intervention. *Freedom from Anger* is a spiritual intervention.

ANGER CAN BE A LIFE-LONG PRISON

Many of us struggle with our anger. We are trapped by it. It is a prison of its own making. It lives within us and keeps us captive to its control. For many of us, this anger is like a cancer that festers and ruins our lives year after year, and we cannot shake it. It controls us. Some know that they are angry, but they just live with it because they don't know what to do about it. Others are unaware of their destructive behavior; they cannot see how there anger flares up and strikes against others, especially those they love.

My dad was harsh. By his words, he struck at me with hurtful blows. But as I look back, he was unaware of his offenses. I grew up to be much like him. I was a yeller. When my children were young—I have nine of them—I found it much easier to yell at them when they frustrated me than to calmly instruct them, discipline them if necessary, and reaffirm my love for them. Yelling seemed to get the result I wanted. They responded out of fear.

I remember with my dad; I used to walk around another route through the house to avoid passing by him. I did not want to subject myself to a potential strike from him with his words. Looking back, I used the same fear tactics with my own children. The scary part is that I, of all people, should have seen what I was doing, but I was blind to it.

We all struggle with anger in some manner, to some degree. We are all captive to our ignorance and our sinful nature.

Jesus came to set us free. The anger itself is only an outcome. The true enemy is deeper within, the roots of which must be healed if we are to be free. Jesus said the devil is a thief, but he, Jesus, came to bring life:

The thief comes only to steal and kill and destroy; I have come that they may have life, and have it to the full. John 10:10

How long must I wrestle with my thoughts and every day have sorrow in my heart? How long will my enemy triumph over me? Psalm 13:2

Isn't that what we struggle with, the battles within? The devil plants the seeds; anger, a consuming weed, springs forth. Our sinful nature is prime soil for anger. When these weeds mature, they wrap their tentacles around us and strangle the life out of us and our loved ones. The weeds grow on the inside of us, but Jesus came to set us free from the inside.

In my anguish I cried to the LORD, and he **answered by setting me free**. Psalm 118:5

We are all prisoners of sin of various kinds. We are all so deeply wrapped up in the trap that we are incapable of releasing ourselves from this formidable enemy living on the inside. We are all in need of someone to rescue us—a Savior. Jesus quoted the prophet Isaiah concerning himself:

"The Spirit of the Lord is on me, because he has anointed me to preach good news to the poor. He has sent me to proclaim **freedom for the prisoners** and **recovery of sight for the blind**, **to release the oppressed**, to proclaim the year of the Lord's favor." Luke 4:18-19

We are prisoners; we need to be set free. We are blind to ourselves; we need recovery of our sight. Anger is an oppressor; it sucks life, peace and hope out of our lives and quenches loving relationships. We need to be released from the oppressor.

Anger can be like an oppressive prison living within us. This study is all about truth. Truth comes from two directions. First, God's Word is truth. God is truth. Jesus is truth. He gave us the Written Word, the Bible, so that we would know his truth. However, there is another important truth, the truth about ourselves. We live with ourselves every moment. We see every thought, every word spoken, feel every emotion and witness every action and reaction. But how well do we truly understand our feelings and motives? Most people do not know what drives them from the inside. Jesus came to bring a light to shine on the inside of each one of us so that the truth about what goes on inside could be revealed. Only when these hidden motives and wounds are revealed does freedom and healing occur.

> Jesus said, "If you hold to my teaching, you are really my disciples. Then you will know the truth, and **the truth will set you free.**"
> **So if the Son sets you free, you will be free indeed.** John 8:31& 36

Honor your father and mother

The devil came in the Garden of Eden to rob mankind of the eternal blessings of the Tree of Life. Through deception he persuaded Eve to partake of the Tree of Good and Evil. His tactics have not changed much. He is still the great deceiver. He is still a thief of life. In the Garden, the devil knew God's words to Adam about not eating of the forbidden tree. He knew the curse of death if they ate of it. He persuasively lied to Eve, convincing her that even though God said they would die if they ate of it, that God was a liar. They would not die; they would be fully capable of blessing themselves.

Satan has enticed man to doubt God's word and to willfully choose a way other than what God commands. But his deceptive work is not finished. He continues to lead us astray into paths of destruction.

The Fifth Commandment says, "Honor your father and your mother"—which is the first commandment with a promise—"that it may go well with you and that you may enjoy long life on earth". Ephesians 6:2-3 The devil knows that if he can bring decay into the family such that fathers and mothers are angry and abusive, that he can set the hearts of their children against their parents such that they will despise their parents, rather than honor them. And they, too, will be robbed of a blessing.

We typically do not honor our parents if they have been abusive to us. And we reap the consequences of not honoring our parents. Our life does not go well. Furthermore, we may become angry abusive parents, just like our own, and the destructive cycle continues, generation after generation. It is a trap that only God can deliver us from!

7

Anger cycle

The following diagram illustrates the anger cycle. This course begins with deep roots of anger that most likely were planted in early years and most likely reveals wounds incurred by someone who should have loved us, like our father. Emotional roots are not quite as deep. They are mostly from our sinful nature, and can be very destructive. Once angry, we may express our anger toward others, hurting them and thereby planting roots in them so that they become angry. We do it to them, and others do it to us—and the anger cycle keeps on going.

ANGER CYCLE: ANGER PROMOTES ANGER

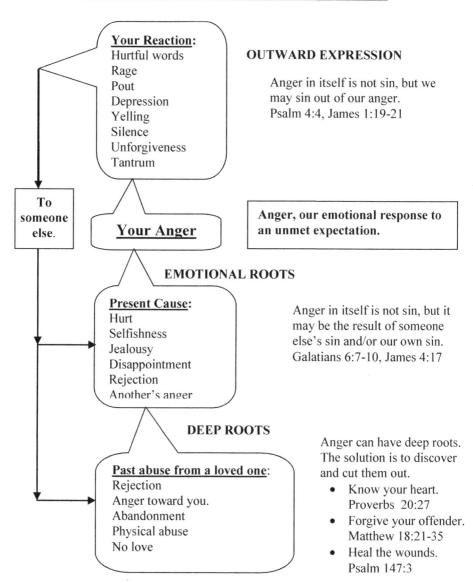

Your Reaction:
Hurtful words
Rage
Pout
Depression
Yelling
Silence
Unforgiveness
Tantrum

OUTWARD EXPRESSION

Anger in itself is not sin, but we may sin out of our anger.
Psalm 4:4, James 1:19-21

To someone else.

Your Anger

Anger, our emotional response to an unmet expectation.

EMOTIONAL ROOTS

Present Cause:
Hurt
Selfishness
Jealousy
Disappointment
Rejection
Another's anger

Anger in itself is not sin, but it may be the result of someone else's sin and/or our own sin.
Galatians 6:7-10, James 4:17

DEEP ROOTS

Past abuse from a loved one:
Rejection
Anger toward you.
Abandonment
Physical abuse
No love

Anger can have deep roots. The solution is to discover and cut them out.
- Know your heart.
  Proverbs 20:27
- Forgive your offender.
  Matthew 18:21-35
- Heal the wounds.
  Psalm 147:3

Reflection questions

We will delve into the roots of our anger in much depth as we progress through this course. The following questions and answers will help each of us see the repetitive nature of anger and the bondage that can occur. We all struggle with these issues at some level, so please begin to share with others for their benefit and your own.

How might your anger have been passed to you?

Was your mother or father angry?

How old were you when you first became an angry person?

Are your children angry? How does anger affect their lives?

How have you not honored your parents? How have you reaped a curse upon yourself because you did not honor them?

Chapter Two

We Are Complex Beings with a Body, Soul, Mind and Spirit

I once knew a loving man who had a very intriguing story about having his soul leave his body. J. Elmer Schmidt has since passed from this life to be with the Lord at 83 years of age. But he almost left this life when he was in his forties. During this time he was experiencing severe anxiety and anger over a demotion in his work. It ate at him for weeks. One day he was hunting in northern Michigan when he experienced a massive internal hemorrhage. He was taken to a small town hospital. They cut him open from top to bottom and pronounced him dead. He said that his spirit left his body and he saw the surgeons cut him open and pronounce him dead. Next he traveled by his spirit all over the hospital, and then he called out to the Lord, saying "Lord, I can't die now; I have four sons to raise." Immediately, he was alive again calling out to the doctors. They had to sew him up again, for they had only used a couple of stitches. This episode changed his entire life.

Obviously, our thoughts and feelings are hidden from others unless we chose to communicate to them by some outward manner, whether it be speech, facial expressions, attitude, etc. After Adam and Eve sinned in the

Garden of Eden, God gave them a covering so that they would not be naked. We normally think of nakedness as uncovering the physical body. But there is another nakedness that we do not normally think about. No one else can see into our minds and see our thoughts. No one can look into my heart and know what I am feeling. Others only see what we choose to show them. I am not certain that before sin that this barrier existed. Actually, there is no need for hidden thoughts, motives, or emotions when there is perfect love, which means there is not sin. There is total trust without any fear when love is made perfect (1 John 4:18, 1 Corinthians 13:4-7).

However, we do live in a sinful world. In fact, not only is everyone we meet a sinner, we are all sinners. Can we trust ourselves? Do we love ourselves? Do we know God's love for us? After all, he is trustworthy; do we trust him?

Many are the woes of the wicked, but **the LORD'S unfailing love surrounds the man who trusts in him.** Psalm 32:10

We go about life thinking that the only one we can trust is ourselves, but our true self that lives deep within our hearts is mostly hidden from our conscious life. Actually, the only one who truly knows the deep things of our hearts is God. Nothing is hidden from God, not our deepest thoughts.

How can this be? How can something be hidden from me when I can see every thought and feel every emotion? Let's look deeper into our makeup.

We are not just biological animals. We are miraculous living physical beings, but we are also thinking beings, and we are spiritual beings. The body, the mind, the spirit and heart of a man all work together as one being. But so much of our being is beyond our understanding. So much of the time we do not understand ourselves. So much is hidden from us, even though we witness every thought and every emotion and every action, much of the time we do not understand the motive.

We Are Complex Beings with a Body, Soul, Mind and Spirit

All a man's ways seem innocent to him, but motives are weighed by the Lord. Proverbs 16:2

Anger comes out of our hearts. We are not a body with a spirit; we are a spirit with a body. (1 Corinthians 15:44b) When these earthly, fleshly bodies give up their life, our spirits will not die with them. Our bodies will stay, but our spirit will go on to eternal existence with God or without him. (Philippians 1:23-24) So who are we inside and how do we work? Do we know our spirit—our hearts? If we are going to deal with our anger, we must begin to understand and know our own hearts. That is where the problem resides. Do we see ourselves as complex beings with a body, a mind and a heart or spirit? They all work together to form one living being.

I am fifty nine years old, and I continually struggle to discover my true motives. For example, I find myself wanting to tell others about what I do. It might be something I built, someone I visited, somewhere that I went, something I heard or saw, a ministry that I have, something that I wrote, etc. I struggle with my motives. Am I just being informative? Am I just being relational? Or am I pridefully drawing attention to me? And if I am, why is that so important? Am I insecure about what people think of me? If so, why? Am I nursing a wounded heart from my youth where I was continually corrected, but rarely affirmed? Maybe all of these motives are present at the same time. It's good to be social and informative, but it is not good to be prideful. So how do I do the good and avoid the bad, especially when I cannot see my true motives.

This example may appear overly introspective, but I think that if we analyze our outward and inward behavior, we will find that there is much about ourselves that is hidden from us. The reason is that we are complex beings with several parts, all working together as a living being. Our bodies are quite obvious. Our minds are equally obvious, but our thoughts are all spiritual—they cannot be weighed, and they have no dimensions, but we know they exist. Feelings are much the same. We are aware of most of our feelings, but we may not be aware of why we feel the way we do. Where does depression and discouragement come from? Sometimes we know we are upset or edgy, but we don't know why. Or, considering that this is an anger course, we may become angry. We may or may not know we are angry. We may know the circumstance that lit the fuse of our anger. But we may not know why we are so easily angered.

We are complex beings with body, soul, mind, heart and spirit. All the parts form one living being. We cannot live without one of the parts.

Analogies:

One: We are like water, salt and sugar. Separately, it is easy to see each one. But when they are mixed together, we know the salt and sugar still exist, but they are hidden in the water, out of sight.

Two: We are like an engine; there is one engine, but individual parts. The fuel system, the lubrication system, the cooling system, the mechanical system—all work together. If one fails, they all fail, yet each part is separate.

The Bible frequently talks about our different parts that make up our being. Notice the different parts: body, soul, spirit, mind, heart.

May your whole **spirit**, **soul** and **body** be kept blameless at the coming of our Lord Jesus Christ. 1 Thessalonians 5:23

Do not be afraid of those who kill the **body** but cannot kill the **soul**. Rather, be afraid of the One who can destroy both **soul** and **body** in hell. Matthew 10:28

Jesus replied: "'Love the Lord your God with all your **heart** and with all your **soul** and with all your **mind**.' Matthew 22:37

Search me, O God, and know **my heart**; test me and know my **anxious thoughts**. See if there is any offensive way in me, and lead me in the way everlasting. Psalm 139:23-24

The **heart** is deceitful above all things and beyond cure. Who can understand it? "I the LORD **search the heart** and **examine the mind**, to reward a man according to his conduct, according to what his deeds deserve." Jeremiah 17:9-10

The heart is the place where our attitudes and motives reside. The heart has thoughts separate from our minds. In fact, the heart may prompt or control the thoughts of the mind.

For **out of the heart** come evil thoughts, murder, adultery, sexual immorality, theft, false testimony, slander. Matthew 15:19

For the word of God is living and active. Sharper than any double-edged sword, **it penetrates even to dividing soul and spirit, joints and marrow; it judges the thoughts and attitudes of the heart**. Nothing in all creation is hidden from God's sight. Everything is uncovered and laid bare before the eyes of him to whom we must give account. Hebrews 4:12-13

For if I pray in a tongue, my spirit prays, but my mind is unfruitful. So what shall I do? **I will pray with my spirit, but I will also pray with my mind;** I will sing with my spirit, but I will also sing with my mind. 1 Corinthians 14:14-15

The LORD saw how great man's wickedness on the earth had become, and that every inclination of the **thoughts of his heart** was only evil all the time. Genesis 6:5

"And you, my son Solomon, acknowledge the God of your father, and serve him with wholehearted devotion and with a **willing mind**, for the LORD **searches every heart and understands every motive behind the thoughts**. 1 Chronicles 28:9a

How well do you know yourself? How well do you know the thoughts of your own heart? Most of us do not know our true self!!! But God does. Jesus is the heart surgeon. [Colossians 2:11, Romans 2:29, Deuteronomy 30:6, Ezekiel 36:25-27] Only through Jesus can we come to know our inner man. Only through Jesus can we come to understand what goes on deep within our heart and soul.

The discussion questions are designed to help us see our complex spiritual nature. In each of these questions, look for the differing functions of the body, the mind and the spirit. Look for how they work together as one being.

[These questions may be done as one large group. If you are the discussion leader, make sure that everyone sees the complex nature in each of these questions.]

Music is obviously physical. It requires a sounding device such as a piano. The sound travels through the air to our ears and our complex hearing system translates the sound into our minds as music. But we also know that music affects our hearts and emotions. If it did not, we would not listen to music. The pleasure of music is the effects upon our hearts. The movie industry is well aware that musical sound sets the spiritual tone of the moment. That is why most movies have a sound track that plays along with the visual and verbal aspects of the story. Music can be used to influence almost any feeling. Music is obviously physical, but it should also be obvious that it is very spiritual in nature.

What about laughter? What is a joke? Why are some funny? Laughter is situational. Mr. Spock from Star Trek was a supposed unspiritual being. He was incapable of feelings. He was incapable of "getting a joke", for this is a process that happens in the heart of a man. It is impossible to program a computer to "get a joke" and rate it's humor. Humor is totally human. And to be totally human requires of us to have a body, soul and spirit. For example, when we see a cute little kid doing something that only two year olds do, we laugh with pleasure. Where does this joy come from? We cannot rationally explain it, but we all are aware of the joyful feeling of laughter it produces.

We Are Complex Beings with a Body, Soul, Mind and Spirit

Where do <u>dreams</u> come from? We all do a very strange thing that we all take for granted. Approximately eight hours each day we all go unconscious. And while we are unconscious, our subconscious (hearts) dream. A fiction writer spends weeks coming up with a creative story line. Dreams create story lines spontaneously, one after another. Those who study dreams tell us that many of the aspects of our dreams are symbolic of real anxieties of our daily lives. Where do all these symbolic representations come from, and how do these dreams minister to our anxieties. We also know from Scripture that God speaks to us through our dreams. Sleep and dreams are a very mysterious spiritual activity.

What about <u>chemicals</u> in our blood such as <u>hormones</u> or <u>drugs</u>. These substances are obviously physical and chemical, but they have the power to affect our emotions, our drives, our attitudes and our actions. These chemicals in our blood stream can turn us spiritually on and off like a switch.

<u>Anger</u> is very similar. Usually it is a physical circumstance that triggers our anger. Much of the time we have a chemical release of adrenaline. The consequence may be a physical display of anger, but there will always be an inward seed of anger that drives our feelings and actions. Where do these seeds get planted? They grow deep within us, then poke up through the soil of our hearts where they can be seen. The roots remain hidden within our hearts.

Reflection questions

The following set of questions may be done in the larger group.

What is music? Does it affect the body or soul?

What is laughter? Where does it come from?

How is anger physical, mental or emotional?

Where do dreams come from?   What is the subconscious?

How do sex hormones affect us physically, mentally, spiritually or emotionally and relationally?   What about drugs?

Where does worry or depression come from? Your mind? Your spirit? Both?

The following questions are for the smaller group.

How well do you understand why you feel the way you do?

When you are offended, what hurts longer, your body or your heart and soul?

Chapter Three

We Were Created in the Image of God

Most of us do not pay much attention or give much thought to the very unique and powerful spiritual nature of man. We were created in the image of God. We were created to have his nature. Sin opposes his nature within us, but the elements of his nature are still there. We are uniquely different from all other living creatures. Let's explore what we are as creations of God, created in the image of God. Our anger finds its source in this unique aspect of our spiritual makeup. To understand our anger, we must first understand who we are as a created being.

We were created in the image of God, but Jesus said that "God is Spirit." John 4:24 Man is not like God because he is physical; he is like God because he is a spiritual being housed in a physical body. This is not to say that our physical bodies do not have any spiritual similarity to God, but it is to say that we do not normally see ourselves as primarily spiritual beings. We cannot see or touch spirits. So when you read the following verses, ponder on how we were created in God's image.

Then God said, "**Let us make man in our image, in our likeness**, and let them rule over the fish of the sea and the birds of the air, over the livestock, over all the earth, and over all the creatures that move along the ground."

So God created man in his own image, in the image of God he created him; male and female he created them. Genesis 1:26-27

RELATIONSHIPS ARE FILLED WITH EMOTIONS

Anger can cause a great deal of damage. We can all identify with a physical outburst of anger. It may be as simple as breaking a pencil in half. It may be more violent by putting a fist through the wall. The damage is regrettable in that the next day we will have to deal with the damage. We will have to buy a new pencil or fix the hole in the wall. But physical damage, even though it is unwanted, is minor compared to the damage that we cause to relationships as an outcome of our anger. Typically, anger is the outcome of a problem in a relationship. And when it comes, we strike out against the other person. It may be physical, usually it is verbal or both verbal and physical. If we hit someone, they will heal in a few days or weeks. But the damage to the heart may last for a lifetime. It will damage the relationship, which will be felt until the relationship is restored, which may never happen.

Our relationships are filled with emotions. This is part of God's design. There is no such thing as an intimate relationship without sharing and risking our emotions with each other. When the relationship is good, the emotions are filled with joy and pleasure. When the relationship is bad, we can be filled with painful emotions, such as jealousy, anger, bitterness, grief, etc. Every relationship is a risk. We cannot control the other persons response in the relationship, so we have to pursue someone and take the risk of his or her response. We have to become vulnerable to others in order to have relationships. It is no different with God. God desires a relationship with us, and he has subjected himself to our love for him or our rejection of him. With the former he receives great pleasure in us. With the latter he receives great pain.

When we get hurt repetitively, we lose our trust in others and put up walls so we will not be hurt again. The walls isolate us, which starves ourselves of love, which we all need to receive and give out. God, on the other hand, does not put up walls. He remains vulnerable to our love or rejection of him. The ultimate demonstration of this openness is found in Jesus Christ.

WE WERE CREATED FOR GOD'S ENJOYMENT

God created the birds, the animals, the fish, the plants and the earth for **man's enjoyment**. (Psalm 115:16) He created man for **his own enjoyment**. God is a personal spiritual being, and since we are created in his image, we are also personal spiritual beings. This makes us capable of having a personal relationship with God.

> Know that the LORD is God. It is he who made us, and we are his; we are his people, the sheep of his pasture. Psalm 100:3

> And the LORD has declared this day that **you are his people, his treasured possession** as he promised, and that you are to keep all his commands. Deuteronomy 26:18 (Isaiah 49:15-16)

WE LOVE BECAUSE GOD IS LOVE

We are emotional beings because God is an emotional being. All men have the need to love and be loved because God is love. We are spirit because God is spirit. (John 4:24). Love is spiritual, and love is man's most basic need. Our relationship with God is based on our loving relationships with one another.

> Dear friends, let us love one another, for **love comes from God**. Everyone who loves has been born of God and knows God. Whoever

does not love does not know God, because **God is love.**   And so we know and rely on the love God has for us. **God is love. Whoever lives in love lives in God, and God in him.**   We love because he first loved us. If anyone says, "I love God," yet hates his brother, he is a liar. For anyone who does not love his brother, whom he has seen, cannot love God, whom he has not seen. And he has given us this command: Whoever loves God must also love his brother.

1 John 4:7-8, 16 & 19-21

GOD KNOWS OUR EMOTIONS

Most of us live our lives unaware of God's presence, unaware of God's concern, unaware of God's understanding of our situations and feelings. In reality, all that we feel is because we have been created in God's image. All that we feel is not foreign to God; he experiences all the pain that we experience. The discussion questions at the end of this chapter aim to reveal how God feels about us, about how special we are to God. Most of our anger is borne out of a problem relationship we have with others. God has a very special relationship with us. We would not have relationships if we were not created in the image of God. Relationships are a basic need of man. It is part of our nature because it is God's nature—we were created in his image.

Since most anger is relational, it is important to understand man as a created relational being. Discover man's special relationship with God through the following discussion questions.

In the next chapter we will study the emotions of God. We were created in his image. We have emotions because God has emotions. This study will help us understand ourselves, specifically our emotion of anger.

We need to see the spiritual side of our everyday life. We need to begin to realize how much our hearts drive our words and actions. How often do we say, "I don't feel like it." when we don't want to do something. Or, "I really feel like....", when we want to do something. Our feelings drive most of what we pursue in life. When people are depressed, they don't feel like doing anything, and they have to decisively make themselves do what they do not feel like doing. Anger is driven by the heart, and there are many strong feelings that drive our actions. In this study we will learn a great deal about where these feelings come from. We will learn about how these feelings can be changed and how we can master them.

God knows our feelings. He doesn't just know them because he can see into our hearts. He knows them because he experiences emotions just as we do.

Loneliness is one of the most painful emotions among man. Does God know loneliness? The Bible does not say directly. However, loneliness comes out of our need to be united with other people. God created man in his image, and he created man with a basic need to be united. God created turtles too. But turtles go about life, all on their own, except for the brief time of mating. Even the young are hatched from eggs and never see their mothers from birth. Not so for man. Babies have a deep need to be nurtured by their mother and to have a strong loving relationship with their father. Among all of God's creatures, only man requires up to twenty years in a family to be raised. And after they grow up, they start their own families, and the families stick together with aunts, uncles, cousins, brothers and sisters and grandparents. God understands families. The Psalmist wrote, "God sets the lonely in families". Psalm 68:6 God has a family (Ephesians 3:14-15), and we are that family. God longs to be united with us. He has called himself our Father, and he calls us his children (1 John 3:1-2, Romans 8:15-16, Galatians 4:6-7).

WE SPEAK BECAUSE GOD SPEAKS

Only man is created in the image of God, and only man speaks and writes. God spoke the universe into existence. Our words are more powerful than we realize.

The tongue that brings healing is a tree of life, but a deceitful tongue crushes the spirit. Proverbs 15:4

The tongue has the power of life and death, and those who love it will eat its fruit. Proverbs 18:21

Jesus is the spoken Word of God (John 1:1&14). This is a very mysterious statement. The spoken and written words of God are part of who God is, just as "God is love". God has given man speech, and we are of God's image because we speak as he speaks. God understands us, not just because he created us, but because he created us in his likeness, his image.

MAN WAS CREATED TO RULE WITH GOD

We frequently talk about going to heaven, yet the Bible says very little in this vane. God has a kingdom, the Kingdom of God. Out of all the creatures, only man will inherit his kingdom (Matthew 25:34, Colossians 1:12-13, James 2:5). Only man will rule with Jesus (Revelation 5:10). Since creation, man has been ordained by God to rule over his creation. Now he has given to us his kingdom to reign with Christ. What an awesome position God has placed us in—what love for mankind!

MAN WAS CREATED AS GOD'S HOME

The Bible tells us that God is making for himself a house made of living stones, and we are that house; we are those stones. (1 Peter 2:4-5, Ephesians 2:19-22, Hebrews 3:6) God created us in his image, and we become the place where he will reside forever. How can one be any more special than that?

God is very much like us in many ways because God created man to be very much like himself. It was his own choice to create man in his own image, the image of God. God has anger, and we have anger because we were created in his image. Because we were created in his image, God understands our anger completely.

Reflection questions

Do you think you can hurt God's feelings? Genesis 6:5-6, Exodus 34:14 How have you hurt his feelings? Why does it hurt him so much?

Why do you think God created us to be like Him?

Chapter Four

Discovering God's Emotions

A nger has many outward behaviors or expressions. It may be violence, yelling, coarse words, etc. Usually we respond to these outward behaviors, yet anger does not find its source in the outward. Rather, the outward behavior is a response to the inward behavior deep within the heart of a man or woman. Anger is very much a spiritual happening.

We normally consider anger as being sinful; therefore God would not have anger. And if he does not have anger, then how can he understand our anger? But a study of God's word clearly describes God as having intense anger. In fact, we have anger because God has anger. We may sin out of our anger. The sin is wrong, but the anger is part of our nature as God created us. Our sin may even drive our anger in the form of a temper tantrum, and that would be wrong. God does not have temper tantrums. Nevertheless, we were created in the image of God. God has anger, and we have anger.

Man is an emotional being because God is an emotional being. There are many emotions, and God can identify with each of them. He understands us!! How well do we understand God? Many of our emotions are also filled with sin and festering wounds. How should we react in

27

emotional situations? Anger is not sin, but we can sin out of our anger. The Bible has a great deal to say about God's emotions, especially his anger. This lesson begins to reveal our true nature and motives by focusing upon God's nature and motives when he is confronted with challenging emotional situations.

Painful emotions can be very difficult for us, such as hurt, anger, discouragement, jealousy and the like. But there are other emotions that we want to bathe in daily, like joy, happiness, hope, peace, feeling loved, etc. Life without emotions would be mechanical, and without life. Our life is filled with emotions because God has created us to inhabit his life, and his life is filled with emotion. Life without emotions is not life!

Let's look at what makes God angry, how he becomes angry, and how he responds out of his anger. But before we do that, let's begin to look at several of God's other emotions, and then, lastly, concentrate on his anger.

WE CAN HURT GOD'S FEELINGS

When we think of God, we think of a being so big, so awesome, so powerful, that he could never be hurt, especially by mere man. We are just a speck in the universe, the universe that God created, and God is much greater than the universe. Certainly we could never hurt him. But let's look at what his own word says about himself.

God formed man in order to have a love relationship. Like any love relationship, we make ourselves vulnerable to each other. God has made himself vulnerable to our love for him. God has been faithful to us, but we have acted like a prostitute in our faithlessness to him. Take the time now to read through these verses to see a glimpse of how we have hurt him in our relationship with him. (Deuteronomy 31:15-18, Jeremiah 2:20-25, 3:1-14, Ezekiel 16:4-42, Ephesians 4:30, Luke 19:41-44)

Sin is anything we might feel, think or do that is against a loving relationship with God or man. When evil flourishes among man, God feels the pain, and the pain is great. Look at how God felt before he destroyed life upon this earth with a flood.

> The LORD saw how great man's wickedness on the earth had become, and that every inclination of the thoughts of his heart was only evil all the time. **The LORD was grieved** that he had made man on the earth, and **his heart was filled with pain**. So the LORD said, "I will wipe mankind, whom I have created, from the face of the earth—men and animals, and creatures that move along the ground, and birds of the air—for **I am grieved** that I have made them." But Noah found favor in the eyes of the LORD. Genesis 6:5-8

God's "heart is filled with pain", when we sin against one another, or when we sin directly against God. When, in our anger, we strike out against our loved ones or we curse God by taking his name, using it in an expression of anger, we sin against man and against God, and God feels the hurt in his heart from the attack against him.

GOD'S DISAPPOINTMENT AND REGRET

We also see from this Flood account that God knows the feelings of disappointment, for he said, "I am grieved that I have made them". God regretted what he had done. God deeply knows our feelings of disappointment or regret. He is well acquainted with displeasure. We have displeasure because we were created in the image of God. Certainly he knows and understands what we feel. Do we know and understand what he feels?! (Also read Matthew 23:37.)

We know that God is all powerful. Nothing is out of his control. He is sovereign, and his will is dominant in all that happens. These verses sound like something was not in his control. We may argue that point, but we cannot argue that he was not pleased with the outcome of man's behavior toward him and among mankind. And his displeasure goes beyond a simple "I'll do it different the next time." God felt intense pain over man's behavior. He took it deeply to his heart. We all know that Jesus suffered for our sins. He almost died in the Garden of Gethsemane due to the intense, deep sorrow over our wayward relationships that alienated us from a committed relationship with God. Jesus spoke of this pain.

"My soul is overwhelmed with sorrow **to the point of death**."
Matthew 26:38

His anguish was so deep and intense that he sweated drops of blood.

An angel from heaven appeared to him and strengthened him. And being in anguish, he prayed more earnestly, and his sweat was like drops of blood falling to the ground. Luke 22:43-44

I cannot even imagine sorrow and anguish so deep that I would sweat drops of blood. If the angels had not come to strengthen him, he may have died in the Garden before making it to the cross. Our heavenly Father weeps with tears over the destructive consequences of our sinful behavior. (Read Jeremiah 8:21-9:1, 13:17 & 14:17)

We may think that Jesus had emotions because he was a man, not because he was God. But Jesus came so that we would know our heavenly Father. He came so that we would see God in him. Jesus was asked to show them his Father, but he said that anyone who has seen me has seen the Father. (John 14:9) Our heavenly Father is a relational being with all of the feelings that go along with relationships. Jesus also said that eternal life was to know our heavenly Father and to know Jesus Christ (John 17:3). To know God we must come to know all of his emotional character. God already knows us; our ambition should be to know God.

God did not have to send Jesus so he could know our pain. God is not tempted by evil. Jesus did come to know our temptations so that he could intercede for us. But he did not come so that he could experience the emotional side of man. God already knows our emotional side. He created our emotional side, and he created us in his image. God is emotional. This is not a weakness, as some would portray emotions. Vibrant life does not exist without emotions. Lets look at a few more of God's emotions.

GOD IS A JEALOUS GOD

We see a picture of God's pain more plainly when we identify with God's jealousy over the people that he created for a relationship with him—and him only. Jealousy is our natural reaction when someone we love—someone who is supposed to be committed to us and us alone—when this person gives themselves to another, jealousy rages like a fire within. God has given us marriage so that we can identify with the relationship that he created us to have with him and him with us. What man or woman would not burn with the pain of jealousy if his/her spouse cheated on them and pursued someone else? God frequently refers to his people as adulterers and prostitutes because they worshipped other gods. (Jeremiah 3:1-5, Ezekiel 16:1-63)

God's jealousy is so much a part of his character that he says that his name is Jealous. Sometimes we take for granted that jealousy is a natural feeling. It is only natural to us because we were created in the image of God, who is a jealous God.

Do not worship any other god, for the LORD, whose name is Jealous, is a jealous God. Exodus 34:14

Another natural outcome of jealousy is anger. We become angry with the one who cheated on us, and we become angry with the one who took our loved one to be their own. God's anger burns against his enemies who come to steal his bride, and he destroys them in his anger. His anger also burns against his loved one, but his love for her is greater than his anger.

How many of us are angry because we have not been loved by those who should have loved us? Was it your father, mother, friend, relative, etc?

GOD IS LOVE

In our human experience, love has many emotions. Think of the feelings of infatuation when we first get a "crush" on someone. We want to spend all of our time with that person, just being together. Think of the loving feelings for a baby or small child, especially your own. Think of the feelings we get from watching a moving love story, whether it be the love of a man and woman, father and child, or deep friends. Love is filled with feelings. But love is much more than feelings. Love is an action word. Love is what we do for others out of our desire for others to have good in their lives. Love is sacrificial. It says, "I will give my life for you so that you will have life."

"God is love." The Bible is filled with verses about God's love (For example: Exodus 20:4-6, Psalm 69:16, 94:18-19, Psalm 103, 106:1, Psalm 107, Psalm 118:1-4, 147:10-11) Man has the capacity to love because he is created in the image of God.

And so we know and rely on the love God has for us. **God is love. Whoever lives in love lives in God, and God in him. We love because he first loved us**. 1 John 4:16 & 19

Most of the problems we have in life involve our inability to love because we have a competing drive that lives within us. It is a drive to serve ourselves first, leaving others to fend for themselves.

Dear friends, let us love one another, for **love comes from God**. Everyone who loves has been born of God and knows God. Whoever does not love does not know God, because **God is love**. This is how God showed his love among us: He sent his one and only Son into the world **that we might live through him**. This is love: not that we loved God, but that he loved us and sent his Son as an atoning sacrifice for our sins. Dear friends, since God so loved us, we also ought to love one another. No one has ever seen God; but if we love one another, God lives in us and his love is made complete in us. We love because he first loved us. 1 John 4:7-12 & 19

Most of our anger is the result of our need for love that is not being met. Most of our anger would be solved if we all loved one another—sacrificially, as God loves us. If we were not created in the image of God, we would not have such a fundamental need to love and to be loved. Much of our anger is resolved when we come to know God's love for us and then begin to love others with his love flowing through us.

A GOD OF PEACE

We all experience turmoil and stress in our lives. We walk around with a tension within us that is about to burst. In fact, for many of us it does burst. We live our lives striking out against others because of the stress that lives within us. Stress can be a major cause of our anger.

I don't think God lives in stress. God knows the opposite—peace. Stress is the result of living with the necessity to be in control, but facing the reality that being in total control is impossible. We foolishly try anyway, and give up our peace. Peace is living in total confidence that God is in control. God is fully capable of being in control. He's God!!!

God is our peace. He knows peace. He wants us to know his peace. It is a peace that is beyond understanding, but when we have it, it feels so good.

Let your gentleness be evident to all. The Lord is near. Do **not be anxious about anything**, but in everything, by prayer and petition, with thanksgiving, present your requests to God. And **the peace of God, which transcends all understanding, will guard your hearts and your minds in Christ Jesus**. Philippians 4:5-7

God is a god of peace (1 Corinthians 14:33, 2 Corinthians 13:11), and Jesus is the Prince of Peace (Isaiah 9:6) We find peace when we trust in the Prince of Peace.

You will keep in perfect peace him whose mind is steadfast, because he trusts in you. Trust in the LORD forever, for the LORD, the LORD, is the Rock eternal. Isaiah 26:3-4

God understands us completely when our hearts and minds are in turmoil and unrest. Not that his heart is filled with turmoil and unrest, but that God is a god of peace, and he is the only source of all peace. Unrest and peace are opposites. The only reason that we can live in either of these states is that we have been created in the image of God. Other animals may experience the stress of the moment, but only man worries and frets about what is happening to him and what will happen in the future.

GOD IS PATIENT

What is patience? Is it just a matter of not being in a hurry? Certainly time is part of much of our impatience. It's also a prompt for much of our anger. We get stuck behind a slow driver and we are late for our next appoint in our packed scheduled day. We start to flare up inside. We say things to the driver ahead of us from our car. We follow behind at two feet. We may flash our lights and honk our horn.

Another sign of impatience comes when we do not get the response out of others that we expected. Our spouse forgot to make the house payment on time. Our child made a stupid mistake on the sports field, so we yell at him from the stands. We try to get through to a business, and all we get are recorded messages, options and buttons to push. <u>Anger flares up when we are not in control—when we don't get what we expect.</u>

We read that "God is love." Well, love is patient and kind (1 Corinthians 13:4). God is patient and kind. He is not in a hurry, and he always wants us to prosper. Time belongs to him—he created it. He does not put time ahead of his loved ones.

> The Lord is not slow in keeping his promise, as some understand slowness. **He is patient with you**, not wanting anyone to perish, but everyone to come to repentance. 2 Peter 3:9

One of the fruits of the Holy Spirit is patience (Galatians 5:22). We were created in the image of God to be like God in his character and behavior. He has given us his Holy Spirit to empower us to live with his character of life.

GOD IS THE SOURCE OF JOY

What is joy? We all know joy in that we would give anything for it. Many will give up all that they have to acquire drugs and alcohol so that they can experience artificial joy. Of course, drugs and alcohol do not bring lasting joy. Actually, they are a counterfeit that, in the end, robs us of all of our joy and replaces it with a trap of deathly misery.

So what is joy? First, let us recognize that there is only one source of joy—God. He has given us his Holy Spirit so that we can have his joy.

> May the God of hope fill you with all joy and peace as you trust in him, so that you may overflow with hope by the power of the Holy Spirit. Romans 15:13

Joy is the inner experience we obtain when we look at the fullness of life that God has set before us. This joyous life is real and has already been given to us by the Holy Spirit.

His Spirit has been given to us now, and many blessings come to us in this life because of the life of the Spirit living within us. But the greatest joy comes when we can see the eternal hope of our eternal future in a kingdom that abounds in life without evil, sin and decay. (Romans 8:18-24) Even Jesus, "for the joy set before him endured the cross" (Hebrews 12:2).

There is a joy that only comes from the Lord. And only man can enjoy his joy, for we were created in the image of God to share in his holiness and joy. The joy of the Lord is our strength (Nehemiah 8:10). [Also read Romans 14:17, 15:13, Hebrews 1:9]

Laughter, happiness and joy are parts of God's makeup. We were created in the image of God so that we could partake of the richness of his character. Sin robs us of these enormous blessings. God wants to bring us back to himself so that we can experience all of these wonderful attributes of God. We are captives in this sinful world in which we live. God wants to bring us out of captivity and into the freedom of his kingdom.

When the LORD **brought back the captives** to Zion, we were like men who dreamed. Our mouths were filled with **laughter**, our tongues with songs of **joy**. Then it was said among the nations, "The LORD has done great things for them." The LORD has done great things for us, and we are **filled with joy**. Psalm 126:1-3

If we could live in this total joy of the Lord, our anger would lose its power over us. We would be set free! God fully knows our predicament—and out of his love for us he has provided a means of escape.

GOD IS GENTLE

Another fruit of the Holy Spirit is gentleness (Galatians 5:23). What is gentleness? Gentleness is an action, something we do. But the actions come from our heart attitude, just like being harsh and overbearing also comes from our heart attitude. God is gentle. We read in 1 Kings 19:11-13 about God's gentleness. God told Elijah to go stand on the mountain in the presence of the Lord.

Then a great and powerful wind tore the mountains apart and shattered the rocks before the LORD, but the LORD was not in the wind. After the wind there was an earthquake, but the LORD was not in the earthquake. After the earthquake came a fire, but the LORD was not in the fire. And after the fire came **a gentle whisper**. 1 Kings 19:11-12

God was not in the powerful wind, nor in the earthquake, nor in the fire. He was in the gentle whisper. God's awesome power produced the wind, the earthquake and the fire, but he came in a gentle whisper. What does this tell us about gentleness? **<u>Gentleness is restrained power under the control of love.</u>** God is not a bully! God does not use his power to throw a temper tantrum. He is like a strong, powerful and huge father who gently picks up his tiny newborn child to softly caress and tenderly kiss him. We read in the Proverbs,

A gentle answer turns away wrath, but a harsh word stirs up anger. Proverbs 15:1

We are going to study God's anger in a moment, but keep in mind that God is gentle. God is not a yeller, as many of us fathers and mothers are at times. God's power is demonstrated in his patience and gentleness.

Through **patience** a ruler can be persuaded, and a **gentle tongue** can break a bone. Proverbs 25:15

A strong, but gentle, word is powerful. Not so a harsh, loud, demanding word. Jesus was gentle (Zechariah 9:9), and he calls us to come and rest in his gentleness.

Take my yoke upon you and learn from me, for I am **gentle** and humble in heart, and you will find rest for your souls. Matthew 11:29

37

> **Describe your patience, peace, gentleness and joy as compared to God's.**

GOD'S EMOTIONS OF ANGER

It is easy to think of anger as sinful—not of God. But God's own Word speaks strongly about God's anger. Is anger wrong? Well, David wrote,

> **In your anger do not sin**; when you are on your beds, search your hearts and be silent. Psalm 4:4

In other words, anger is not necessarily sinful, but we can sin out of our anger. God's anger is righteous. Keep in mind that God is sovereign, and we are just men, created by our sovereign God. However, even considering God's sovereignty, if we could manage our anger as God manages his anger, we would be much less likely to sin out of our anger. David also wrote,

> O LORD, do not rebuke me **in your anger** or discipline me in your wrath. Psalm 6:1

David had asked the Lord to be gentle with him, not to vent his anger on him, even if it was deserved. But David also asked the Lord to exercise the wrath of his anger on all his enemies, especially the nations who were enemies to God's people.

> Arise, O LORD, **in your anger**; rise up against the rage of my enemies. Awake, my God; decree justice. Psalm 7:6

> How long, O LORD? Will you be angry forever? **How long will your jealousy burn like fire?** Psalm 79:5

We see from these verses that God does have anger, and is prompted by two motives. First, he is angered by his own loved ones when they rebel against him, seek out other gods to worship and reject his love. Second, his anger also rages against all of his enemies.

We are commanded not to sin in our anger. We see that in God's anger he is under certain restraints. He is not out of control, just to vent his anger—his emotions. He acts upon his anger to produce a certain righteous outcome. We would do well to do the same. Let's take a closer look at certain aspects of God's anger so that we may learn from him, our creator. If we can model his behavior, we may be successful to obey the command, "In your anger, do not sin."

GOD'S ANGER AROUSED BY HIS LOVED ONES

God is typically portrayed as a judgmental deity that created a bunch of rules for us to follow, and because we break his rules, he is ticked off and wants to inflict his wrath upon us. This view is in gross error because it completely misses the love relationship between God and man.

God's anger is aroused by his jealousy.

We have already learned that God is a jealous god. In fact, he says that his name is Jealous. Jealousy also implies that God longs to have a committed loving relationship. He commits himself to be faithful and trustworthy, and he expects his loved ones to be committed and faithful to him in this love relationship, this marriage between God and man.

When man begins to flirt with other lovers, gods of a different making, God's anger is aroused by his jealousy.

Fear the LORD your God, serve him only and take your oaths in his name. Do not follow other gods, the gods of the peoples around you; **for the LORD your God, who is among you, is a jealous God and his**

anger will burn against you, and he will destroy you from the face of the land. Deuteronomy 6:13-15

How angry would you be if your spouse was sleeping with your neighbor? Your anger would be two fold: You would be angry with your spouse for being unfaithful, and you would be angry with your neighbor for stealing your wife. That is just how God feels when we stray from our love relationship with him by pursuing all of the pleasures of the world, and all this when God is offering us true, perfect life that flows from him without cost. He becomes angry with his wayward wife, and he becomes angry with his enemies, the ones who enticed his loved ones to come sleep with them. This anger is good. How loved would you feel if you slept with your neighbor and your spouse was not hurt and didn't care? What would that say about his love for you, or the lack of it?

God's anger can burn against his loved ones when they reject him.

God had just delivered his people from over 400 years of bondage and slavery to the Egyptians. He sent Moses to deliver them. He performed ten miraculous plagues against Pharaoh of Egypt. He parted the Red Sea so they could escape the ensuing Egyptian army, and then he drowned the army in the sea as it collapsed in on them. He provided Manna, quail and water for them in the desert. He provided a cloud of shade from the hot desert sun and fire at night to keep them warm. He provided the Promised Land that was flowing with abundance. In spite of all his love, provision and protection, they did not trust God. They grumbled and complained that God would leave them to be killed by their enemies, to starve and die of thirst.

God's people continually denied and rejected God's love for them, and they stirred up his anger toward them. While Moses was on the mountain as God gave him the Ten Commandments on stone, the people were worshiping a gold calf in wild revelry. If it was not for Moses interceding for them in their behalf, God would have completely destroyed them in his anger.

"I have seen these people," the LORD said to Moses, "and they are a stiff-necked people. Now leave me alone so that **my anger may burn against them** and that I may destroy them. Then I will make you into a great nation."

But Moses sought the favor of the LORD his God. "O LORD," he said, "why should your anger burn against your people, whom you brought out of Egypt with great power and a mighty hand? Why should the Egyptians say, 'It was with evil intent that he brought them out, to kill them in the mountains and to wipe them off the face of the earth'? **Turn from your fierce anger**; relent and do not bring disaster on your people. Exodus 32:9-12 (Also see Deuteronomy 9:18-21)

God's anger can be aroused by our disobedient unbelief in his promises and his love for us. (Numbers 11:1-3, Mark 3:1-5)

God has chosen to give us victory over our enemies. He has promised to go ahead of us, to empower us to fight victoriously. He sends us forth to do his bidding. In the end, he gives us the victory. We are the ones who reap the blessings. But will we believe him when he calls?

One day Moses saw a burning bush in the desert that did not burn out. As he approached it, God spoke to him from the bush. He told Moses that he was to go to Pharaoh and tell him to let his people go. Moses was fearful, but the Lord said he would go with him. He promised, "I will stretch out my hand and strike the Egyptians with all the wonders that I will perform among them." Moses still complained in unbelief, so God told Moses to throw his staff down, and it turned into a snake. Then he told him to pick it up, and it turned back into a staff. Then he told him to put his hand in his cloak, and when he took it out, it was covered with leprosy. He put it back in and out again, and it returned to normal. God promised to turn water from the Nile River into blood on the ground.

You would think that talking to God in a burning bush, having him make all these miraculous promises and demonstrating his power would give any man the confidence to obey God and go forward in his commands. But Moses still did not trust God.

But Moses said, **"O Lord, please send someone else to do it."**
Then the LORD'S anger burned against Moses ... Exodus 4:13-14
(Read the entire account: Exodus 3&4)

God is not some mean old ogre who makes a bunch of rules and then waits to see if someone breaks them so he can pounce on them. He is a God that loves us. "God is love." He desires to rescue us, to empower us, to flow through us. He desires a deep loving relationship with us. His anger is aroused when we do not believe him and reject his love for us.

God is quick to forgive, slow to become angry.

God's anger is not aroused by impatience, frustration, temper tantrums, unexpected circumstances, etc. His anger flares up because his loved ones have gone astray and because his enemies have stolen his bride and perverted his creation.

God's anger is not rash and instantaneous. He is slow to anger, and his anger is always tempered by his incomprehensible love. He may be angry with us for our rebellion against his love and his sovereignty, but his compassion for his loved ones is even greater. We may have rejected him. We may have run off with other lovers. But he wants us back, and he is quick to forgive. He is willing to pay whatever the price to get his wayward adulterous wife back.

The LORD is compassionate and gracious, slow to anger, abounding in love. He will not always accuse, nor will he harbor his anger forever; he does not treat us as our sins deserve or repay us according to our iniquities. Psalm 103:8-10

(Also read Exodus 34:6-7, Psalm 30:5*, Psalm 60:1, Psalm 78:38-40*, Psalm 85:3-7*, Psalm 103:7-14*) (* verses included in discussion questions.)

Man's anger is aroused by many of the same inputs. Our anger can flare up when a loved one offends us in any of a number of ways. However, unlike God, we have a nature that easily breeds bitterness. We are quick to become angry and slow to forgive. Our anger would be short-lived and would not grow such deep destructive roots if we were under the control of love rather than our self-seeking flesh.

God mourns over our sin against him and our rejection of him.

Man naturally allows his anger against others to fester, bringing about a deepening separation. We see divorce at an all time high. Once close relationships can be broken with a lifetime of bitter division. Wounds from a parent during childhood can fester late into life, even after parents have been dead and gone.

God's heart is not that way. He always agonizes over broken relationships with his children. He longs for them to come back to him. It is not God who rejects us; it is man who rejects God. It is not God who remains distant; it is man who remains aloof. Jesus looked on to Jerusalem, just hours before they were to totally reject him, slander him, torture him and take his life on the cross. He looks over the people who have always betrayed and rejected God, and he weeps over them.

"O Jerusalem, Jerusalem, you who kill the prophets and stone those sent to you, **how often I have longed to gather your children together, as a hen gathers her chicks under her wings, but you were not willing.** Matthew 23:37

If our hearts were like God's, always looking for a way to restore the broken relationship—if our hearts were like his, our anger would not fester. It would not consume us. And our relationships would come alive.

God's anger burns toward his enemies.

It would be a huge mistake to think that God's anger is no big deal, nothing to be concerned about, since we know that he is slow to anger and quick to forgive. God is an awesome foe to his enemies. In the end, all of his enemies will be destroyed by his fierce anger. We should tremble at his anger toward his enemies.

If we deliberately keep on sinning after we have received the knowledge of the truth, no sacrifice for sins is left, but only **a fearful expectation of judgment and of raging fire that will consume the enemies of God**. Hebrews 10:26-27

God's anger has always been something to fear by those who oppose him. These words were sung by the Israelites on the shore of the Red Sea right after God drown the Egyptian army in the sea. The people rejoiced in God's outpouring of anger.

In the greatness of your majesty you threw down those who opposed you. **You unleashed your burning anger; it consumed them like stubble**. Exodus 15:7

We, too, should rejoice in God's anger against all our enemies, particularly the devil and the world he reigns over. The devil is out to "steal and kill and destroy" us (John 10:10). He is like a roaring lion, prowling around seeking a chance to devour us (1 Peter 5:8). God's anger toward our enemies is a very good thing. God is all powerful, and he applies his power in anger to deliver and protect us.

44

We don't normally think of Jesus as having anger, but think of how he chased the money changers out of the temple with a whip, turning over their tables. (Mark 11:15-17)

We were all once enemies of God, subject to his intense wrath. But even then, God provided a way for us to be transformed from enemies to sons of God. (Read Romans 5:6-11 and Colossians 1:21-23)

The discussion questions all deal with God's anger. Appoint a secretary to take notes during your discussions. As you go through each verse, discover attributes about God's anger. See how many points you can discover in each scripture reference. Seek to see God's anger in light of his love. How does his love affect his anger? Check off these attributes as you find them from the following list. Some are found more than once.

Reflection questions

God's chosen people were continually rescued from their enemies by God. God continually blessed them. Yet, in spite of all his love for them, his people complained about God; they did not believe his promises for them. Like an adulterous wife, they worshipped other gods, hurting him and arousing his jealousy and anger.

Discuss the following verses and <u>write down</u> what you discover about God's anger from each verse.

Deuteronomy 6:13-15

Psalm 30:5

Psalm 78:36-42, Psalm 78:56-59

Psalm 79:5

Psalm 85:3-7

Psalm 103:7-14

God's anger attributes:

- His jealousy arouses his anger.
- His anger is short-lived.
- He is patient, and not easily angered.
- He will endure much abuse and pain before allowing his anger to develop.
- His anger is controlled; it does not control him. It is not irrational.
- His anger is tempered by his desire to forgive and to have mercy.
- He is slow to anger.
- His anger is always tempered by his love.
- He does not harbor, or hold onto his anger, as many of us do.
- God has made himself emotionally vulnerable to us, and he does not put up protective walls to protect himself, like most of us do.
- His response to his anger is compassion because he loves us and he wants our relationship to be restored above all. (This leads into the next lesson.)

Chapter Five

God's Compassion: The Power to Forgive from the Heart

Deep rooted anger resides in a wounded, offended heart. It is a bondage that does a great deal of damage to the beholder. It not only torments him, but his angry behavior wounds, offends and torments those around him, especially his family members. The cause of his anger is typically the result of growing up with someone who had the same wounded, offended and tormented heart. Consequently, a wounded father will wound all those around him. His sons and daughters will grow up with the same wounds that afflicted their father. When they marry and have children, the same wounds will get passed on to their children through the same unloving behavior that wounded them.

The outward behavior from these wounds comes in a variety of destructive relational behaviors. It may be violent anger where family members are physically attacked and furniture is broken. It may result in terribly abusive language where very hurtful words are spoken, and much yelling is practiced. It may be in a host of rejecting attitudes where everyone is blamed for Dad's misery. It may be in the form of abandonment, workaholism, alcoholism, controlling behavior, drug additions, unfaithfulness, depression, demonic behavior, etc. It may be deviant behavior, sexual abuse, crime and imprisonment. All of these can come out of a wounded, angry heart that can fester for a lifetime—long after the original offenses are past.

The bondage and destruction will go on for a lifetime if not released. Release from this horrible bondage requires forgiveness, but just knowing that we need to forgive does not necessarily empower us to forgive and be released. We need compassion for our offenders. Compassion for those who offend us empowers us to forgive and set us free. This compassion is important for forgiving the sins of those who should have loved us in our past, but it is also critical for walking in forgiveness on a daily basis toward all those around us. People who are holding onto offenses from childhood will find that they are continually offended by every little disturbance or minor mistreatment. They will be offended by their employer, their supervisor, their spouse, their children, relatives, their neighbor, the government, anyone in public who they think should be serving them, etc. They constantly complain about how someone else is abusing them and taking advantage of them. They are in a huge trap that they cannot see, nor do they believe it exists. All they know is that they are miserable, and it's everyone else's fault.

When we fall victim to these wounds, we lose much of our ability to love others. <u>Ironically, loving others is our way of escape from this trap that has engulfed us. Release comes when we can forgive those who offended us.</u> The power to forgive comes from a heart of love for our offenders. This love is motivated out of our compassion for our offenders. Our offenders are in the same bondage in which we find ourselves. This becomes a circular trap. Who will set us free? Our loving heavenly Father has sent Jesus to empower us with compassion so that we can forgive from our hearts and be set free from the trap that holds us tight, that controls our lives with internal and external destruction.

GOD'S COMPASSION FOR HIS WAYWARD PEOPLE

God is a god of compassion. Our need to be compassionate does not come from our own powers and makeup. It comes from our almighty compassionate God. We were created in the image of God. Our entire makeup was designed and created by God. Sin has robbed us of our godly nature, but God desires to restore us so that we live our lives directed by his heart in all things. Compassion is God's nature. He desires to equip us with his compassion for others—especially those who should have loved us, but instead they abused us. God knows what it is like to be subject to abuse by the ones who were supposed to love him. He knows what it is like to pour out his love, only to be rejected by those he loved. God has compassion for us, and he provides the ability to be compassionate to others through Jesus Christ.

God's compassion for us empowers our compassion for others. "Love covers a multitude of sins." (1 Peter 4:8) It is good to see God's compassion. We can model his compassion, but more importantly, we are empowered to have compassion for others when we see the compassion God has for us.

Compassion is our love response to the ones we love who may have hurt us, who have sinned against us. God knows what it is like to have his loved ones reject him, to sin against him. Let's begin by examining his loved ones. How does God see man? God has a love affair with us, his people. We were created for his very special purposes. Look at some of the relationships that God has with us, and we have with God as found in the Bible.

- **We are his children.** 1 John 3:1-3, Ephesians 5:1
- **We are his lover-his wife.** Ephesians 5:22-33
- **We are his chosen ones.** 1 Peter 2:9-10
- **We are the body of Christ.** 1 Corinthians 12:27
- **We are his house or temple.** Ephesians 2:19-22
- **We are his kingdom, his nation.** Exodus 19:3-6, Revelation 1:6, 5:9-10

Clearly, we are not just expendable creatures that God uses as pawns. We are his prized, loved children who will inherit the riches of his kingdom. We are the "apple of his eye". (Psalm 17:8, Deuteronomy 32:10, Zechariah 2:8)

In spite of these special relationships given to us by God, we have cheated on him, rejected his love and purposes for us, and we have pursued other lovers and other kingdoms. Yet, he still wants us back, and he is willing to pay any price for us. In fact, he was willing to give the life of his only son, Jesus Christ. That's compassion.

Typically, the ones who arouse our anger most are the ones we expected to love us the most.

Jesus gave a parable that has been coined "The Parable of the Lost Son". (Luke 15:11-32) Using this title directs the focus on the runaway son. I think there is another major focus in this parable. Let me suggest a new title, "The Parable of the Loving Compassionate Father". This parable is a picture of our Father in heaven. Take the time now to slowly read through this parable, looking for the compassion that the father had for his son that took his wealth and squandered it on wild living. When he came to his senses, he realized how much his father provided for him. He humbly returned to his father. You would think that his father would have been stirred with anger toward his son for rejecting his love for him and for wastefully and sinfully spending his wealth. But that is not the case. Look at the following excerpt from this parable. Notice that it says, "while he was still a long way off, his father saw him and was filled with compassion for him; he ran to his son, threw his arms around him and kissed him." He saw him while he was still a long way off. The son had been gone for quite a few days by this time, maybe even a year or so. But his father looked out every day, hoping to see his son coming back. His heart was heavy for his son. He looked out in the distance each day to see if this was the day that he might return. When he saw him, he didn't just wait for him to come to the house; he ran to him, hugged him and kissed him. He raised him up as his

50

precious son. He threw a great celebration because his lost son had returned to him. The offense was not on his heart. The love for his son dominated his being, and he overflowed with compassion. **There was no place for anger!**

So he got up and went to his father.

"But while he was still a long way off, his father saw him and was filled with compassion for him; he ran to his son, threw his arms around him and kissed him.

"The son said to him, 'Father, I have sinned against heaven and against you. I am no longer worthy to be called your son.'

"But the father said to his servants, 'Quick! Bring the best robe and put it on him. Put a ring on his finger and sandals on his feet. Bring the fattened calf and kill it. Let's have a feast and celebrate. For this son of mine was dead and is alive again; he was lost and is found.' So they began to celebrate. Luke 15:20-24

Notice also that this son had a brother who had not run away. But he had no compassion for his lost brother who now returned. He even disowns him by refusing to refer to him as his brother, but as "this son of yours". We are also much like the son who stayed home. In our pride we think that we have been perfect. We see the sins of others, but we cannot see our own downfalls. All of our sin against one another is also against God. God is quick to forgive out of his compassion for us, yet we are selfish, and we see everything from a self-serving point of view. Our hearts are naturally hard toward others and our compassion is buried, or nonexistent. We need the compassion of our heavenly Father so we will become empowered to love and forgive. The returning son found freedom in his Father's love. The stubborn son who stayed home was in deep bondage. He had lost all of his joy by holding onto his pride and false self righteousness.

We need the compassion of our heavenly Father, so let's study his compassion in more detail to see what it is like.

God's compassion is sacrificial, as a parent for a child.

It is no mistake that we call God our heavenly Father. And it is not a trivial claim that we are the children of God.

How great is the love the Father has lavished on us, that we should be called children of God! And that is what we are! 1 John 3:1

A father or mother does not just forget about their own child—no matter what he has done. A rebellious child may arouse the anger of his father, but that does not mean that he stops caring about his welfare. A normal parent never stops loving his child. God is more than a normal parent. "God is love." His love is unending. We are precious in his sight no matter what we have done. When we sin and rebel against him, he weeps for us. He does not write us off and forget about us. Our names are always before his eyes.

Shout for joy, O heavens; rejoice, O earth; burst into song, O mountains! For **the LORD comforts his people and will have compassion on his afflicted ones**. But Zion said, "The LORD has forsaken me, the Lord has forgotten me." "Can a mother forget the baby at her breast and have no **compassion** on the child she has borne? Though she may forget, I will not forget you! See, **I have engraved you on the palms of my hands**; your walls are ever before me. Isaiah 49:13-16

God's compassion, out of love, never closes the door for reconciliation.

God is sovereign. He is not a pushover. He does not overlook our sinful behavior. If he did, he would not truly love us, for what parent does not care about the behavior of their children. However, just as a deeply loving parent, when we return to God, no matter what we have done, he accepts us back. His compassion is great. Our offenses toward him do not reduce the love and concern that he has for us.

> **If you return to the LORD**, then your brothers and your children will be shown compassion by their captors and will come back to this land, for the LORD your God is gracious and compassionate. **He will not turn his face from you if you return to him."** 2 Chronicles 30:9

Notice that he does not turn his face from us. In other words, he does not just allow us to crawl back to him with conditional love from him. He welcomes us back into an intimate relationship—face to face. It is the face of God that ministers to us and saves us from our fallen lives (Psalm 31:16 & 80:3). He never holds back from accepting us and coming close to us.

For us, when we are rejected by our loved ones, we typically withhold our blessings. We get hurt feelings, and we react out of our hurt. God gets hurt feelings too, but he does not walk in rejection. He desires reconciliation and restoration. He is willing to pay the heavy price of reconciling his relationships with his children—he sent his Son to die for us in order to get us back. There is no greater sacrifice, no greater price. God loved the children of Israel. He rescued them from their enemies. He protected them and provided for them. He gave them a future with incomparable blessings. Yet, they rebelled against God and pursued other gods for their blessings. How would we react in this situation? How do we react when someone rejects us? God was angry, but he never stopped loving, and his compassion for them resulted in keeping an open door for their return. Let's look briefly at the account.

> "But they, our forefathers, became **arrogant** and **stiff-necked**, and did not obey your commands. They refused to listen and failed to remember the miracles you performed among them. They became **stiff-necked** and in their **rebellion** appointed a leader in order to return to their slavery. **But you are a forgiving God, gracious and compassionate, slow to anger and abounding in love**. Therefore you

53

did not desert them, even when they cast for themselves an image of a calf and said, 'This is your god, who brought you up out of Egypt,' or when they committed awful blasphemies.

"**Because of your great compassion you did not abandon them** in the desert. By day the pillar of cloud did not cease to guide them on their path, nor the pillar of fire by night to shine on the way they were to take. **You gave your good Spirit to instruct them.** You did not withhold your manna from their mouths, and you gave them water for their thirst. For forty years you sustained them in the desert; they lacked nothing, their clothes did not wear out nor did their feet become swollen. Nehemiah 9:16-21

God's anger can be greater than any anger we have ever witnessed. But his compassion is equal or greater in comparison. He is not just an angry god, looking for a reason to destroy his wayward loved ones. He is a loving, patient, forgiving and compassionate God, always ready to restore our relationship.

Much of the time our anger is aroused by every tiny event or offense that it seems we are just looking for something to be angry about. Compassion and reconciliation are last on our minds.

God's compassion forgives over and over for the same offense.
(Psalm 51:1-2)

Jesus told his disciples,

"If your brother sins, rebuke him, and if he repents, forgive him. If he sins against you seven times in a day, and seven times comes back to you and says, 'I repent,' forgive him." Luke 17:3-4

We usually can forgive someone once, but what if the offense occurs again and again? How easy is it to have compassion toward the one who continually repeats his offense? God's people continually rebelled against him. Year after year, millennium after millennium, they disobeyed and sought out other gods. But God continued to receive them back out of his great compassion for them.

"But they were disobedient and rebelled against you; they put your law behind their backs. They killed your prophets, who had admonished them in order to turn them back to you; they committed awful blasphemies. So you handed them over to their enemies, who oppressed them. But when they were oppressed they cried out to you. From heaven you heard them, and **in your great compassion you gave them deliverers, who rescued them from the hand of their enemies.**

"But as soon as they were at rest, they again did what was evil in your sight. Then you abandoned them to the hand of their enemies so that they ruled over them. And when they cried out to you again, you heard from heaven, and **in your compassion you delivered them time after time.** Nehemiah 9:26-28

God is long-suffering, meaning that his love is sacrificial. He is willing to suffer for our welfare, even if the suffering comes from our rebellion and cheating against him. Compassion always looks past the offenses against us.

Compassion comes out of true love for the one who rejected our love.

God is love. We typically think of love as a good feeling toward someone, but love is an action word. Love is sacrificial and filled with decisive principles. Look at some of the direct definitions of love given by Paul in 1 Corinthians 13:4-7.

- Love "always protects.
- Love "always perseveres".

55

- "Love never fails."
- Love "is not easily angered."
- Love "keeps no record of wrongs."
- Love is "patient and kind."

God's compassion for us is driven from his love. If we are to have compassion so that we are not easily angered, being patient and kind, and keeping no record of the wrongs against us, then we need to be filled with God's love. All love comes from God; therefore, compassion also comes from God.

Compassion is the love of a father for his wayward son, and we are his sons and daughters.

Compassion comes from a binding commitment. God has given us our own children so that we can have some understanding of his compassion for us. Many children reject their parents love. They rebel and go their own way, denying anything good from their parents. Most parents do not reject their children, even when their children reject them. Instead, they agonize over their wayward life, always desiring a change of heart so that their lives would be blessed. This is how God's compassion is for his wayward children. Our rebellion against his loving ways may arouse God's anger, but his compassion never fails to desire good things and a change of heart. We already looked at the story of the "Compassionate Father" in Luke 15:11-32. God is not an angry old ogre. He is our heavenly Father who loves his children with deep compassion.

The LORD is compassionate and gracious, slow to anger, abounding in love. He will not always accuse, nor will he harbor his anger forever; he does not treat us as our sins deserve or repay us according to our iniquities. For as high as the heavens are above the earth, so great is his love for those who fear him; as far as the east is from the west, so far has he removed our transgressions from us. **As a father has compassion on his children, so the LORD has compassion on those who fear him; for he knows how we are formed, he remembers that we are dust.** As for man, his days are like grass, he flourishes like a flower of the field; the wind blows over it and it is gone, and its place remembers it no more. But from everlasting to everlasting the LORD'S love is with those who fear him, and his righteousness with their children's children—with those who keep his covenant and remember to obey his precepts. Psalm 103:8-18

"For a brief moment I abandoned you, but with deep compassion I will bring you back. In a surge of anger I hid my face from you for a moment, but with everlasting kindness I will have compassion on you," says the LORD your Redeemer. "To me this is like the days of Noah, when I swore that the waters of Noah would never again cover the earth. So now I have sworn not to be angry with you, never to rebuke you again. Though the mountains be shaken and the hills be removed, yet my unfailing love for you will not be shaken nor my covenant of peace be removed," says the LORD, who has compassion on you. Isaiah 54:7-10

Is not Ephraim my dear son, the child in whom I delight? Though I often speak against him, I still remember him. **Therefore my heart yearns for him; I have great compassion for him," declares the LORD.** Jeremiah 31:20

We see from these verses that we have rebelled against God and aroused his anger, but his love and compassion for us is not cast aside because of our rejection of God's involvement in our lives. He still longs for us back as a father to a son—and more so, more than we can know or imagine.

When we come back to God, he is quick to receive us, for he is longing for the day of our return. (angels rejoice over one that is

saved.)   God   even   has   compassion   for   his   enemies. Micah 7:18-19, Zechariah 10:6

We all know the story of Jonah and the whale. God had asked Jonah to go to Nineveh, the capital of Assyria, and preach repentance. The Assyrians had been fierce enemies of the Israelites for years. Jonah hated the Assyrians. He knew that if he preached repentance, and if they repented, God would have compassion and mercy on them. Jonah ran from his calling because he did not want to see them receiving God's mercy, love and compassion.

God eventually had his way with Jonah, and Jonah did go to Nineveh and preach repentance. The entire city of about 200 thousand repented in just three days. And God delighted to have mercy on them, to forgive their sins out of his compassion for them. But Jonah was angry with God for being so compassionate. Jonah's anger was aroused because he did not have the same compassion as God.

When God saw what they did and how they turned from their evil ways, **he had compassion** and did not bring upon them the destruction he had threatened.But **Jonah was greatly displeased and became angry**. He prayed to the LORD, "O LORD, is this not what I said when I was still at home? That is why I was so quick to flee to Tarshish. I knew that **you are a gracious and compassionate God, slow to anger and abounding in love, a God who relents from sending calamity**. Now, O LORD, take away my life, for it is better for me to die than to live."

But the LORD replied, **"Have you any right to be angry?"**
Jonah 3:10-4:4

At one time we were all enemies of God. Thank God for his great compassion for us that he gave up the life of his son so that we could live. Now it is our turn. We are obligated to have compassion for others out of thanks to God for his compassion for us. (Colossian 1:21-23)

God loves his bride so dearly that he is willing to forgive her for selling herself to other lovers. God does not pursue a divorce. He longs for reconciliation.

Divorce today runs about one divorce each year for every two marriages per year. Marriages do not start out with the intent of divorce. Offenses take place that are deemed intolerable, and the relationship is ended. God sees us as his spouse. All that he has ever desired is for his wife to be faithful to him. There is no other husband as loving and caring as God, yet his bride has longed for other lovers. There are many verses like the following, describing how we have sought out the world in place of our heavenly husband who longs to provide all good things for us.

"'How weak-willed you are, declares the Sovereign LORD, when you do all these things, **acting like a brazen prostitute!** When you built your mounds at the head of every street and made your lofty shrines in every public square, you were unlike a prostitute, because you scorned payment.

"'**You adulterous wife! You prefer strangers to your own husband!** Every prostitute receives a fee, but you give gifts to all your lovers, bribing them to come to you from everywhere for your illicit favors. So in your prostitution you are the opposite of others; no one runs after you for your favors. You are the very opposite, for you give payment and none is given to you. Ezekiel 16:30-34

The Israelites pursued every foreign god. They even set up places to worship them right within the temple. This would be like coming home and finding your spouse in bed with your neighbor. Worse yet, what if you invited your husband/wife to watch while you made sexual love with the neighbor next door. This is the kind of hurt we have laid upon our Lord by seeking out all the pleasures and provisions of the world, and all the while passing by our Lord for his loving provisions. But God is not quick to divorce. He has great anger, but his love is everlasting, and he is driven by his compassion to get his wife back for his own.

59

We do not naturally respond as God responds. We are quick to divorce, to end the hurtful relationship. God's love for us does not stop with our offenses. His love is never ending. His compassion for us does not degrade due to our pursuit of other lovers. He wants his bride back, and he will pay the price for her.

"How can I give you up, Ephraim? How can I hand you over, Israel? How can I treat you like Admah? How can I make you like Zeboiim? **My heart is changed within me; all my compassion is aroused. I will not carry out my fierce anger, nor will I turn and devastate** Ephraim. For I am God, and not man—the Holy One among you. **I will not come in wrath.** Hosea 11:8-9

We know the price he paid for us. He gave the life of his only Son, Jesus. God's love and compassion for his wayward wife are more than his anger and wrath.

We have severely offended God, yet he has compassion and mercy for us. He longs to restore the relationship. He is willing to suffer for it.

MAN'S COMPASSION FOR THOSE WHO HURT US DEEPLY

When this series is taught in a classroom, the testimony of David Meece, "Forgiving my father" is played from a CD. David Meece is a gifted Christian song composer of the 1980's era. He grew up in an extremely abusive household. His father was an angry alcoholic who routinely beat his mother and threatened the children. David refers to him as an "angry drunk". But worse than his physical abuse was his verbal abuse. David recalls the last words he heard from his father; as his father pointed a gun at David's forehead he said, "You're worthless!!" David hated his father. David became a well-known Christian music artist. And while he ministered to others, he rotted away inside. He hated his father. At one point God revealed to him how much he hated his dad and he knew that

60

he had to forgive him. But he couldn't. He spent two years going to all sorts of "How to Forgive" classes. But he still hated his dad, and maybe even worse because now he thought about it all the time. Stuffing the negative emotions, memories and thoughts does not make them go away. They are still fully alive deep within us. And they still have the power to directly influence our lives in how we act, feel, perceive and relate to others.

David struggled for two years trying to forgive his dad. Finally, one day the Lord intervened. In a private moment, David saw his dad in a vision. He knew it was his dad, but he saw him when his dad was a little boy. He also saw that this little boy had also been abused as David was by this little boy when he grew up. He saw all the hurt and the pain and the rejection and the hopelessness of this little boy, who was his father. David began to hurt with him, and all he wanted to do was to put his arms around him, hug him and tell him that he loved him. God had given David compassion for the father who abused him. And at this point he could forgive his father.

God is a compassionate god. Compassion comes out of love, and "God is Love." Our compassion comes out of love. Our love and our compassion come from God. When we struggle to forgive, we need for God to give us compassion so that we will have the power to forgive from our hearts. It is important to make up our minds to forgive from our minds, but forgiving from the heart is a work of the Lord's power within us. It still requires submissive obedience, but the power comes from the Lord.

It is highly recommended that you get a copy of David Meece's testimony. This writing does not, and cannot, present the full impact or content of his message. You can get it from Focus on the Family (1-800-A-FAMILY or www.family.org). The name of the CD is "Forgiving My Father" with Mr. David Meece (CD 162/29578).

Reflection questions

How has God had compassion and mercy toward you?

Describe your feelings of compassion toward the one who has offended you the most.

What would happen to your anger toward someone if you decided to give him your undeserved mercy?

Chapter Six

Commanded to Be Compassionate

A s already expressed, the power to be compassionate comes from the Lord. But we have already received his Holy Spirit so that we have this power living within us. Scripture commands us to be compassionate toward others. Not just those who have seriously offended us from the past, but we are to walk in compassion in our daily relationships.

Compassion is both an empowerment that comes from the Lord and an act of obedience that comes from our will. This is true for most spiritual choices in our lives. We are empowered to love by the Holy Spirit that God has given us, but each time we love we make a choice to sacrifice something of our lives for another's life. Jesus is the prime example. Our heavenly Father loved us long ago, but he made a choice to sacrifice his only Son so that we would have his life. Compassion is both an empowerment from God as well as a choice of obedience.

Compassion for a father who seriously abused us will likely require God to give us a divine revelation and love for our offender. This may be expected for one or two people from our past where the abuse has caused deep scars. However, take a broader look at life. We are offended nearly every day by loved ones, friends, associates and even enemies. We cannot walk around holding bitterness toward all those people—waiting for God to give us divine insight so that we can forgive and unite. In most of these relationships we are to have compassion as an act of obedience.

At this point, let's define two important properties of our forgiving attitudes.

> **COMPASSION:** **Feeling the sufferings and struggles of another, especially for the ones who offended us—love for your offender.**
> **MERCY: Not enforcing the penalty for the debt of a sin out of love —decisive forgiveness.**

Having compassion and mercy can be a discipline of choice. We can decide to look at our offender and deliberately focus on this person to know who he is. This requires of us to focus on him rather than ourselves. This requires of us to come close to him, even if he is not willing to come close to us. It means that we will ask questions of him and listen to what he has to say, listening intently with our hearts so that we can understand where he is coming from. It means withholding judgment. It means overlooking offensive behaviors.

When we walk in compassion and mercy toward our offenders, our anger is diffused and love takes over.

Compassion comes from a heart-felt desire to restore a relationship because we love them. The love is a choice on our part. When something happens in life that drives a wedge between us and someone else, we should be the ones to devise a way to restore our relationship. Our sinful nature is one that pouts and puts the reconciliation burden on the other person. But if we want to act like our loving creator, we should be the ones to seek out the estranged person.

God does not take away life; instead, he devises ways so that a banished person may not remain estranged from him. 2 Samuel 14:14

God, our heavenly Father, sent his Son in the likeness of man so that we could be reunited with him. His Son was sent to make atonement for our sins. We don't have to atone for ourselves, even though we are the offending party in our relationship with God. Jesus is the one who goes before our Father on our behalf, interceding for us. He was made like us so that he would have compassion on us, so that he would know what it is like to be tempted, so that he could help us in our temptations. God understands what goes on inside us. He understands why we offend him. And he sent Jesus so that he could restore our relationship.

For this reason he had to be made like his brothers in every way, in order that he might become a merciful and faithful high priest in service to God, and that he might make atonement for the sins of the people. Because he himself suffered when he was tempted, he is able to help those who are being tempted. Hebrews 2:17-18

For we do not have a high priest who is unable to sympathize with our weaknesses, but we have one who has been tempted in every way, just as we are—yet was without sin. Hebrews 4:15

Compassion is a choice on Gods part. He could have destroyed us and started over. He is fully capable of doing that. He did not send Jesus in order to salvage his hard work of creating us. It isn't his hard work that he is trying to salvage; it's his bride that he wants back. He sent Jesus because he loves us and he wants us back. Compassion is a choice of love. That's compassion, and we are to do the same when we relate with one another.

At this point it is important to realize that compassion is not an option; we are commanded to be compassionate toward those who sin against us.

The following verses very clearly command us to have compassion and to forgive those who offend us. This is a matter of putting love into action. God has had compassion for us. He sent his Son to die for us so that our sins would be forgiven and so that we would receive his Holy Spirit to live within us, empowering us to love, have compassion and to forgive as he has done for us.

Our compassion for others should model God's compassion for us. Jesus was sent out of God's compassion. Now we should become like Jesus, having his attitude toward all people.

If you have any encouragement from being united with Christ, if any comfort from his love, if any fellowship with the Spirit, if any tenderness and compassion, then make my joy complete by being like-minded, having the same love, being one in spirit and purpose. Do nothing out of selfish ambition or vain conceit, but in humility consider others better than yourselves. Each of you should look not only to your own interests, but also to the interests of others.

Your attitude should be the same as that of Christ Jesus: Philippians 2:1-5

God's Word to us clearly commands of us to be compassionate and merciful.

Get rid of all bitterness, rage and anger, brawling and slander, along with every form of malice. **Be kind and compassionate to one another, forgiving each other, just as in Christ God forgave you.** Ephesians 4:31-32

Therefore, as God's chosen people, holy and dearly loved, **clothe yourselves with compassion, kindness, humility, gentleness and patience. Bear with each other and forgive whatever grievances you may have against one another. Forgive as the Lord forgave you**. And over all these virtues put on love, which binds them all together in perfect unity. Colossians 3:12-14

Finally, all of you, **live in harmony with one another; be sympathetic, love as brothers, be compassionate and humble. Do not repay evil with evil or insult with insult, but with blessing, because to this you were called so that you may inherit a blessing.**
1 Peter 3:8-9

Do not repay anyone evil for evil. Be careful to do what is right in the eyes of everybody. If it is possible, as far as it depends on you, live at peace with everyone. Romans 12:17-18

Speak and act as those who are going to be judged by the law that gives freedom, because **judgment without mercy will be shown to anyone who has not been merciful. Mercy triumphs over judgment!**
James 2:12-13

Blessed are the merciful, for they will be shown mercy. Matthew 5:7

Reflection questions

What is your first reaction when someone offends you—to retaliate or to reconcile?

When was the last time you showed compassion and mercy for your offender?

What grudges are you holding toward those in your life (family, neighbors, work associates, Christians, etc.)?

PREPARATION FOR THE NEXT LESSON:

Much of the time we are unaware of who is in need of forgiveness. When our hearts have been severely wounded, we set up protective walls to keep from being hurt even more. Sometimes we get so used to being hurt as we continue to live in a hostile environment that we are not sensitive to the offenses that have accumulated. The pain and injury may be so great that the only way to live with it is to deny that the offenses exist. We all need to be loved. Sometimes we lie to ourselves by denying the lack of love that exists. Denial is not compassion! Denial is not forgiveness! Jesus said that he came that we might know the truth and that the truth would set us free. Jesus is truth. Jesus is the Word, and the Word is truth. Truth is seeing all things as they truly exist. Jesus came that we might have his light within our hearts to reveal the truth about our hearts.

The following worksheet should be used privately. It is not meant to be shared with anyone in class. It is a tool for you to meditate and pray and to allow the Lord to reveal where you are harboring hidden wounds and unforgiveness. When you discover them, ask God to give you compassion, to reveal his love for you and to heal your wounds.

PERSONAL FORGIVENESS WORKSHEET

Who has angered you? How have you been hurt by someone who should have loved you?

Who do you hold unforgiven?   <u>**Make a private written list of their names. This is a critical exercise.**</u>

Possibilities for harboring anger against a parent:

- Physical abuse (hitting, sexual).
- Yelling.
- Their anger.
- Legalism: Work for love. Conditional love. Work for approval. Rules without affection or value just for being a son or daughter.
- Addictions: alcoholic, drugs, gambling, pornography.
- Abandonment (total, married to job, lived for recreation, lonely house).
- Zero affirmation, rejection.
- They complained, argued and were unhappy, possibly depressed.
- Harshness, cutting words.
- Critical and discouraging (Colossians 3:21)
- Selfish, uncaring and unfair.
- Workaholic.
- Divorce.
- Unfaithness to spouse (affairs, etc.)
- Father/mother did not care for the family.
- I was given too much parental responsibility to hold up the household.
- Divisions between father and mother.
- Lack of love between mother and father.
- Homelife was absent.
- Strong parent(s), but little tenderness, compassion, joy, and love.
- Favoritism for other child(ren).

- Too much discipline.
- Too little discipline (You were a brat. You still are a brat. Now you are insecure. Hebrews 12:7-11)
- I was spoiled.
- Did not bring me up in the training and instruction of the Lord. (Eph. 6:4)
- Did not protect me, defend me or rescue me.

Possibilities for harboring unforgiveness against someone other than a parent:

- Jealousy.
- Envy.
- Slander and gossip.
- Offensive or harsh words.
- Unfaithfulness.
- Rejection.
- Theft.
- Physical harm.

Have you forgiven yourself?

- Lost years and wasting life
- Offending your children
- Ruining your marriage
- Failing in life
- Broken relationships
- Running from God
- Anger, drug and alcohol addictions, gambling, crime

Chapter Seven

Forgiveness, a Direct Offense and Major Weapon against Anger

Do you know that we live on a battle field? This life is an intense battle between the kingdom of darkness as led by the devil and the kingdom of light as led by Jesus.

Think of the conflict that rages between men every day. On the larger scale, there are always one or more wars going on someplace on earth. What is war? A nation of people rises up against another nation of people. They each use weapons to fight against each other until one side overpowers the other. The intent is to destroy the property of and take the lives of fellow human beings until they are so weakened that they can be consumed.

At a slightly smaller scale we have the constant fear of terrorist attacks. Men plot in darkness how they can surprise a nation with an evil destruction of property and innocent lives.

At a smaller level we have crime. Our prison population continues to grow in order to control crime. Crime is defined by murder, theft, rape, selling illegal drugs, etc. Crime is an individual offense against an individual or society. It is the act of willfully inflicting harm on another person, ether to his person or his property.

Some of us fall victim to some of the above. Some of us are the perpetrators of the above. But there is another level where we all become perpetrators and victims. We all strike out against someone else in one fashion or another. It may be in violent acts, but most of the time it is through our everyday words and actions. We get upset with someone and we speak words to that person with the intent of causing emotional harm. We may be unfaithful to a relationship, deeply wounding the other's heart and violating their trust. We may be the one who is always on the taking end, and rarely the one to give. We are talking about sin. Love is when we put the needs of others ahead of ourselves. Sin is when we put our own desires ahead of others—even to the point of taking of their welfare for the sake of our own.

This is the battle between the two kingdoms. The devil is referred to by Jesus as the "prince of this world" (John 12:31, 14:30 & 16:11). The devil heads the kingdom of darkness. Jesus is the King of the Kingdom of Light. All of us give our allegiance to one of these two kingdoms, even if we are unaware of our choice. All of us were born into the devil's kingdom, the dominion of darkness. It is only because of Jesus that some of us come out of this dark kingdom and enter into Jesus' kingdom that is filled with the light of life.

> …giving thanks to the Father, who has qualified you to share in the inheritance of the saints in the **kingdom of light**. For he has rescued us from the **dominion of darkness** and brought us into the **kingdom of the Son** he loves, in whom we have redemption, the forgiveness of sins. Colossians 1:12-14

The devil is a thief, and he comes to rob us of all life. Jesus came so that we would have his abundant life within us.

> The thief comes only to steal and kill and destroy; I have come that they may have life, and have it to the full. John 10:10

Forgiveness, a Direct Offense and Major Weapon against Anger

The devil has many schemes to keep us in darkness. He is a master deceiver. Jesus called him the "father of lies" (John 8:44). He is a master at temptation. He tempted Eve with a lie, and she believed him. He tempted Jesus, who refuted his lies with the written Word. And he tempts us. One of his greatest schemes is to lead us into an offense against someone such that the offended person offends back. The two are held in unforgiveness— a bondage that is stronger than prison bars. The thief traps us in unforgiveness, and in so doing cuts off this abundant life that Jesus brings. When Jesus was asked to teach them to pray, he gave a prayer, which we have called The Lord's Prayer. Look at what is in the middle of this prayer.

Forgive us our debts, as we also have forgiven our debtors. And lead us not into temptation, but deliver us from the evil one.'
Matthew 6:12-13

Forgiveness, fleeing from temptation and being delivered from the evil one—the devil—are critical for a fruitful life on this earth.

This battle between kingdoms goes on even if we are unaware of it. In fact, that is part of the devil's tactic, to keep us unaware of the war and his schemes. If we are unaware, then he can go about his evil business without opposition. We fall right into his evil plots without any warning, and we suffer in his grip without knowing that we have fallen captive. In fact, in our ignorance, we blame ourselves and others for our bondage.

Most of us go through life unaware of the intense spiritual battles all around us. These battles involve our inner selves, but they also involve all the relationships that we have with others. To make it more complicated, we have an enemy, the devil, who is invisible to us, but who is very present. Peter said, "your adversary the devil walks about like a roaring lion, seeking whom he may devour." 1 Peter 5:8 (NKJV) He works hard to make sure that we offend one another, and that we readily take offense and walk in unforgiveness. Unforgiveness produces all sorts of destructive consequences. It festers into bitter roots within our hearts that not only destroys our relationships, but it destroys our own lives as well as those around us. Jesus defeated the devil on the cross, but how was this done? He did not retaliate against those who slandered, tortured, lied about and killed him. Instead he asked God to forgive them because they did not know what they were doing. His giving up the right to retaliate and his forgiveness for his offenders brought about the defeat of the devil (Colossians 2:13-15, 1 John 3:8). Our victory is not different; we need to forgive.

FORGIVENESS IS A SPIRITUAL WEAPON AGAINST ANGER AND AGAINST THE DEVIL'S SCHEMES

Battles are fought with weapons. The advancement of warfare is the advancement of weaponry. It is no different with spiritual battles, other than the weapons are not physical, but spiritual. Paul described this battle.

For though we live in the world, **we do not wage war as the world does. The weapons we fight with are not the weapons of the world. On the contrary, they have divine power to demolish strongholds.** We demolish arguments and every pretension that sets itself up against the knowledge of God, and we take captive every thought to make it obedient to Christ. 2 Corinthians 10:3-5

It would be simple if we could see our enemy, but our enemies are powerful spiritual forces. If we are to come against them we must first be aware of them and their schemes. Then we must arm ourselves for battle. Just because we cannot see them with our eyes or reach out and touch them with our hands does not mean they are not there. Paul described our true enemies.

Finally, be strong in the Lord and in his mighty power. Put on the full armor of God so that you can take your stand against the devil's schemes. For our struggle is not against flesh and blood, but against the **rulers**, against the **authorities**, against the **powers of this dark world** and against the **spiritual forces of evil in the heavenly realms**. Ephesians 6:10-12

When I was a kid I was afraid to go down in the basement at night. I wasn't sure what was lurking behind the furnace. I went from room to room, quickly turning on the lights. Many of us have a real fear of being out at night in a strange place. And our fears may be well warranted; many evil things occur at night. We fear what might be hiding in the darkness, what might strike at any time. We fear because we know that many of these fears are real. All we have to do is read the newspaper to hear about the terrible things that do happen, and could happen to us if we were not aware.

Well, these "rulers", "authorities", powers of this dark world and "spiritual forces of evil in the heavenly realms" are very real. And as the scripture says, we should "take our stand against the devil's schemes". What are his schemes? He has many, but instilling bitterness and unforgiveness toward another is one of his most powerful schemes against man. If he can cause an offense (sin) and then convince the offended to hold onto the offense, he has trapped both the offended and the offender. What is our weapon against this scheme? First, we should not sin against one another. But offenses are going to happen, even when they are not intended. Our weapon of spiritual warfare is to forgive. Forgiveness is power over this unseen enemy. Again, look at what Paul said about the devil's schemes and our victory over them.

If you forgive anyone, I also forgive him. And what I have forgiven—if there was anything to forgive—**I have forgiven in the sight of Christ for your sake, in order that Satan might not outwit us. For we are not unaware of his schemes.** 2 Corinthians 2:10-11

We must become keenly aware of unforgiveness. When we are angry with someone, it is time to open our spiritual eyes and see what is happening. The devil is taking advantage of your life and your sinful fleshly nature.

"In your anger do not sin": Do not let the sun go down while you are still angry, and **do not give the devil a foothold.** Ephesians 4:26-27

Some offenses are deep and deliberate. Our powerful weapon is still forgiveness. Many offenses are minor, and we should overlook them.

It is to his glory to overlook an offense. Proverbs 19:11

All of us struggle to varying degrees with our sensitivities. Many times we take offense toward someone for things that were done with no ill intent whatsoever. The wrong words may have been used, which gave rise to a misunderstanding and offense. Maybe everyone was invited to an occasion, but your name was mistakenly forgotten. Maybe an accident causes you harm or loss. If we readily walk in forgiveness, the offense will cause no harm to the relationship—whether the offense was intentional or not. If we readily take offense, a division will occur, and the devil gains a foothold. If not resolved, he will gain a victory. Let us not be fools to his schemes and give him the victory!

Forgiveness is more than just addressing our feelings or another's feelings. Forgiveness is breaking spiritual bonds of spiritual death. Forgiveness is one of our most powerful spiritual weapons. Forgiveness heals and restores. Unforgiveness divides and destroys.

WE DECIDE TO FORGIVE

We may say, "But I just can't forgive." We say this as if we are powerless to forgive. But how powerless are we? I think the real issue lies within our belief that we are justified in our unforgiveness. We also act in unbelief regarding the consequences of our unforgiveness. First, we are not powerless; we have been given the Holy Spirit. **Forgiveness is a work of the Holy Spirit and carries with it the full authority of God.** (Mark 2:1-12, John 20:22-23)

76

Forgiveness is a decision that we make for ourselves. We don't just wait until we feel like forgiving. We forgive decisively out of obedience. Much of the time it seems like we just can't do what we want to do. And I believe that most of these times our inhibition is not our inabilities; it's our lack of a decision. We want something, but we have not decided to do it because we are unwilling to pay the price of our decision. We want it to come easy, and we are unwilling to sacrifice if it comes hard.

How many of us want to lose some fat? We try all kinds of diets that allow us to eat without going hungry. But we still do not lose weight. We go for a walk to burn off some calories, and then fill up our plate at a pot-luck. The decision to lose weight is a decision to be hungry several hours per day without feeding our bodies. It's dying to our flesh. This is true for most everything that is controlling us through our flesh. If we make a decision to suffer, we can reign over our flesh. If we don't make this decision, the flesh remains on the throne. Peter wrote,

> Therefore, since Christ suffered in his body, arm yourselves also with the same attitude, because **he who has suffered in his body is done with sin**. As a result, he does not live the rest of his earthly life for evil human desires, but rather for the will of God. 1 Peter 4:1-2

This is true for overeating, smoking, drinking, drugs, getting out of bed, procrastinating hard work, etc. It is also true for forgiveness. We must make a decision to forgive and suffer whatever it is that we must give up in order to release the other person.

WE FORGIVE OUT OF OUR FEAR OF THE LORD

Forgiveness for others is a requirement for being a Christian. It is a requirement for our own forgiveness. It is the mark of a Christian. Jesus was quite clear.

Forgive us our debts, as we also have forgiven our debtors. And lead us not into temptation, but deliver us from the evil one.'

For if you forgive men when they sin against you, your heavenly Father will also forgive you. But if you do not forgive men their sins, your Father will not forgive your sins. Matthew 6:12-15

These are very weighty words from Jesus. I think that if we truly believe what he said, forgiveness would not seem so impossible for us. "But if you do not forgive men their sins, your Father will not forgive your sins." In other words, if I do not forgive others who sin against me, I will not be forgiven and I will spend eternity separated from God in a place of darkness and torment. If I truly believe Jesus' words, then forgiveness should not be so impossible for me. It may be very sacrificial, but not impossible. That is why the Scriptures speak so strongly about the fear of the Lord.

—**continue to work out your salvation with fear and trembling,** for it is God who works in you to will and to act according to his good purpose. Philippians 2:12-13

He will be the sure foundation for your times, a rich store of salvation and wisdom and knowledge; **the fear of the LORD is the key to this treasure**. Isaiah 33:6

The **fear of the LORD is a fountain of life**, turning a man from the snares of death. Proverbs 14:27

The fear of the LORD is the beginning of wisdom; all who follow his precepts have good understanding. To him belongs eternal praise. Psalm 111:10

The fear of the Lord is a good thing. Without it, it is unlikely that we will walk in obedience—in all things, but especially in this area of forgiveness.

This is more than a legal requirement; it is fundamental to our relationship with God and man.

Forgiveness is an act of obedience for sure. And the consequences of deciding not to forgive have eternal considerations. This ought to motivate us to forgive at all costs. But there is a motivation that goes beyond obedience and the fear of the consequences.

At this time read Matthew 18:21-35.

FORGIVENESS IS A DECISION TO SUFFER OUT OF LOVE FOR GOD AND OUR OFFENDER

Forgiveness on God's part was an unimaginable sacrifice for both our heavenly Father and for Jesus. We focus on Jesus' bodily suffering, but his Father suffered too; he gave up the life of his only son. And the suffering of Jesus' body was only part of his suffering. He took upon himself the sins of the whole world. What does that mean? Romans 6:23 says, "The wages of sin is death." Sin is like cancer; it eats away at the very fabric of life. Jesus took this deathly disease of our sin upon himself and suffered the death consequence of our sin. He paid the heavy price for our forgiveness.

Forgiveness is "carrying our cross daily". Jesus was put on the cross by sinner's sin. He did not have to suffer; he chose to suffer out of love for us. We are instructed to take up our cross in the face of sinners. We are to love our enemies.

And he said, "The Son of Man must suffer many things and be rejected by the elders, chief priests and teachers of the law, and he must be killed and on the third day be raised to life."

Then he said to them all: "If anyone would come after me, he must deny himself and take up his cross daily and follow me. For whoever wants to save his life will lose it, but whoever loses his life for me will save it. Luke 9:22-24

Jesus suffered death on his cross at the hands of sinful men. Men sinned against Jesus, but he did not retaliate—as he could have, but rather he allowed men to sin against him. Peter drew his sword in the Garden of Gethsemane, but Jesus rebuked him. He said he could call upon his Father to send twelve legions of angels, but he chose to suffer at the hands of man rather than to annihilate them (Matthew 26:52-53). Upon his cross—dying and being mocked by the crowds—he asked his Father to forgive them because they did not know what they were doing (Luke 23:34). He instructs us to face the same cross in our lives. Taking up our cross daily is the decision to forgive rather than take offense and retaliate when someone sins against us. It is commonly stated, "Hate the sin; love the sinner." But when you love a sinner, he will likely sin against you. It is one thing to overlook a sin from a distance—without being sinned against. It is another thing to love someone enough that we are willing to come close and subject ourselves to their sin. And then, when the sin evolves, allow it to happen without retaliation, rejection or bitterness. Forgiveness is an act of love. It covers over sin.

Hatred stirs up dissension, but love covers over all wrongs.
Proverbs 10:12 (1 Peter 4:8)

Jesus teaches us that we should love our enemies. Read Matthew 5:38-48 now.

Yes, we should forgive because we fear the Lord and the consequences of not forgiving. But in our hearts we should forgive because it is right, because our hearts are filled with the love of God—the same love that he

80

had for us when he gave up his life so that we could live. We should forgive out of thankfulness and humility before our Lord who died for us.

We must have a bigger perspective. Forgiveness is the walk of a Christian. Forgiveness is the only answer to sin that is taking us under. Without forgiveness we live with division, resentment, grudges, bitterness, back-biting, slander continual offenses—and anger. **Without forgiveness, we cannot unite as one body.**

Therefore, as God's chosen people, holy and dearly loved, clothe yourselves with **compassion**, kindness, humility, gentleness and patience. **Bear with each other and forgive whatever grievances you may have against one another. Forgive as the Lord forgave you. And over all these virtues put on love, which binds them all together in perfect unity.** Let the peace of Christ rule in your hearts, since as members of one body you were called to peace. And be thankful. Colossians 3:12-15

FORGIVENESS HEALS THE WOUNDS

We live in a world of sinners. With the exception of Jesus, every man and woman that has ever lived, lived as a sinner. Every child ever born was raised by sinful parents. All family members are sinners. All your neighbors are sinners. All your work associates and everyone you see on a daily basis—are all sinners. Sin is an offense against someone. We live in a world where offenses happen among <u>all</u> people. When we are offended, we become wounded to some degree. When wounded, we can respond in a variety of ways. We may become angry and retaliate. We may withdraw. We may feel rejected. We may become bitter. Our relationships become damaged and we become isolated from our loved ones.

What is the solution? There are two: We could all stop sinning right now, all at once. Of course, that is an unreasonable expectation, even if just for our self. We cannot control someone else's behavior, but even if we could control our own and alleviate all sin, others would still be sinning against us. The wounds would still run deep and continuous. Even if we all could stop sinning all at once, we would still have the past hurts and wounds. So this first solution is really not a solution.

The second solution is to forgive. When Jesus returns and we are all transformed into the likeness of Jesus in the "twinkling of an eye", then all sin will stop and we will all be healed from the inside out. But what do we do in the meantime while we are all still sinners? Forgive!!! Forgiveness releases us from the offenses of another so that the sin may still hurt, but the outcome is not a wound. Forgiveness is an act of love. As God's word teaches us,

Hatred stirs up dissension, but **love covers over all wrongs**. Proverbs 10:12

He who covers over an offense promotes love, but whoever repeats the matter separates close friends. Proverbs 17:9

Above all, love each other deeply, because **love covers over a multitude of sins**. 1 Peter 4:8

<u>**Anger in itself is not sin, but it can be the result of someone else's sin or our own sin. The sin cannot be undone, but forgiveness can totally heal the wounds to you or to others.**</u>

For now, forgiveness is all we have. Forgiveness delivers us from emotional bondage, restores relationships, and heals the wounds of our hearts.

Forgiveness begins in our hearts, but forgiveness is not a private matter. The offense began with a relationship. Forgiveness is relational.

Confession is walking in the light. Forgiveness flows from the light. (1 John 1:5-10) We harbor bitterness in dark private places. We receive healing of bitterness when we confess it. When we are holding on to bitter unforgiveness, our entire attitude toward others changes into one of cynical criticism. We tend to see ourselves as victims, not just to the one who initially offended us. We see ourselves as victims of our employers, victims of the government, victims of anyone in authority, victims of the church, etc. If allowed to fester, the whole world around us becomes our enemy. We see the world through wounded eyes. And when we do this, the wound festers and grows larger. Healing does not come through complaining about our perceived enemies. Healing comes through confession of our bitter unforgiveness.

> And the prayer offered in faith will make the sick person well; the Lord will raise him up. If he has sinned, he will be forgiven. **Therefore confess your sins to each other and pray for each other so that you may be healed**. The prayer of a righteous man is powerful and effective. James 5:15-16

We forgive and love because we love God for all that he has forgiven us. He came for our healing, now we are to walk in his healing forgiveness out of our love for God. Do we know how much we have been forgiven?!!!

The Pharisees were bitter against Jesus. They had no cause. Jesus came for people. He healed the sick. He drove out evil spirits. He accepted the lowly and downtrodden. He loved sinners, no matter what they had done. The Pharisees, in their prideful insecurity, looked down on others, judging the severity of their sin, and in so doing did not see their own depravity.

One day a Pharisee invited Jesus to his house. While he was there a woman came who had been involved in many sinful behaviors, but Jesus had accepted her out of his deep love for her and ministered to her and had forgiven her. She came into the Pharisee's house to bless Jesus. She anointed him with her expensive perfume and washed his dirty, stinky feet with her tears and her long hair. The Pharisees looked down on her for her sins and spoke against Jesus for allowing this sinner to love him. But Jesus saw deeply into this woman's heart and into the hearts of the Pharisees, and he told them,

Therefore, I tell you, her many sins have been forgiven—for she loved much. But he who has been forgiven little loves little." Luke 7:47

When we hold onto bitter unforgiveness, we continually reject sinners, and we are blinded to our own sin, which grieves the Lord. The more we hold onto our bitter grudge, the less we can see the loving mercy that God has for us. And the less we know of God's love for us, the deeper our bondage to bitterness.

Bitterness is a leading cause of anger. It is one of those roots that must be cut out if we are to have victory over anger. Forgiveness is a decisive action that cuts out our bitter roots.

Bitter root: The seeds of unforgiveness germinate, sprout and grow deeper and deeper, consuming the life of its beholder.

Bitter roots are growing tentacles of unforgiveness that suck the life out of its victim which destroy all loving relationships. Each tentacle seeks to offend others so that more roots can be planted and more victims claimed.

Further study:
Vengeance: Romans 12:17-21, 1 Peter 3:8-9
Asking and seeking forgiveness: Matthew 5:21-26 & 18:15-17
Our words reveal our heart: Matthew 12:34-37 & 15:18

Forgiveness is not optional; it is commanded of us. The Scriptures are very clear. Jesus was very clear. Forgiveness is an act of obedience. Forgiveness is a weapon against our true enemy, the devil.

Get rid of all bitterness, rage and anger, brawling and slander, along with every form of malice. Be kind and compassionate to one another, forgiving each other, just as in Christ God forgave you. Ephesians 4:31-32

See to it that no one misses the grace of God and that **no bitter root grows up to cause trouble and defile many.** Hebrews 12:15

I have forgiven in the sight of Christ for your sake, in order that Satan might not outwit us. For we are not unaware of his schemes. 2 Corinthians 2:10-11

Reflection questions

How could forgiveness be a weapon against anger in your life?

What bitter or bad feelings or negative thoughts are you carrying toward someone? What bitter roots are you fertilizing?

What is your inner response to someone who offends you?

Are you easily offended? What angers you the most about others? What is your "button"?

How do you know when you are holding someone in unforgiveness?

Chapter Eight

Angry with Your Life

We have already learned that all of us have a capacity for anger because we were created in the image of God. We have also learned that we can become angry out of our own sinful nature. All sin is wrong, and we can have unrighteous motives and actions that are driven by our anger.

We have also learned that we can become angry because of the way others have treated us. This is especially the case if we were abused by a loved one in our formative years. This does not make our anger right or redemptive. Forgiveness is the release from this bondage, and we are commanded by God to forgive.

There is another serious source of our anger that can be related to the abuse in our formative years, or even later in life. Many are angry with their life. They feel their life is ruined and without purpose or hope. Their life is filled with frustration and with no obvious resolution.

This anger can come from an unlimited number of sources. You may be sick or injured. You may be crippled or in pain. It may be that you cannot live out your life as you naturally expected. You cannot do the things that most other people do. Your handicap limits your ability to provide for yourself. It may be that you struggle for money—for survival. Or you do not have the friends that other normal people have because you cannot socialize with them in the manner they do with each other.

You may have fooled around in your teen and early adult years. You may have wasted those years when you should have been pursuing training for a career. Now you are strapped with responsibilities and it appears too late to go back. Now you are stuck for the next forty years with little hope for an enjoyable, prosperous career.

There are many life situations that "pull the carpet out from under us". Your spouse may have divorced you. You may have been fired from your job and now you cannot find employment. You may have acquired a physical ailment that cripples your body and life. You may have been convicted of a crime and now your "good life" has been exchanged for a prison sentence. You may have an addictive habit like drugs, alcohol, smoking, overeating, etc. that controls your life. You are depressed and hopeless because of it, but now that you feel so bad, you go back to the addiction, thinking that it will comfort you.

You may not like yourself, and you think that others think lowly of you. Your parents may have been the ones who told you that you were worthless, or at least treated you in a manner that conveyed that you were not valuable to them. They may have been perfectionists, critical and condemning in their words and actions. All of this added up to your perception of yourself, even though it is a lie. Now you feel terrible about yourself. Your attitude cripples you such that you either fail at most things, or you never feel that anything you do is good enough. Life is one big frustration. You are depressed and angry.

Much anger is outward against someone else. But a closer look may reveal that you are very angry with yourself, your life or your situation. This anger toward yourself then reflects with anger into all of your relationships.

[The group should first answer the following questions, and then gather again for instruction regarding hope for your lives.]

> **How are you angry, regretful or frustrated about your life?**
>
> **How are you discouraged or depressed? Do you feel your life is out of your control?**
>
> **What do you think of yourself?**
>
> **How are you angry with God or yourself about your life? Have you forgiven God and yourself?**

ALL TRUE HOPE IS IN GOD

The true source of all hope is in God. There are many today whose hope is in themselves, their situation, their job or status, other people, etc. The only true and lasting hope is a hope in God. It is the only hope that will not fail us. Be of good hope and cheer, for God loves you. He has a plan for your life. He has not forgotten you or forsaken you. He is working in your life, even now. Trust him! He desires for you to come to him and to be used for his Kingdom purposes. We were born into a dark world; our true life is in God's kingdom.

This may sound like something that is easy to say by someone who is not suffering, but trying to understand the love of God in the midst of suffering can be discouraging in itself. Many Christians suffer in many ways. They may pour their hearts out to God, but their deliverance does not seem to come. Let's take a closer look at suffering and hope.

Let's separate our suffering into two groups: physical and spiritual. For example, if we are suffering from an illness or handicap. That is the physical part. Along with this may come depression, loneliness, discouragement, hopelessness and anger. That is the spiritual part, which is the hardest to bear.

PERSEVERING HOPE IN GOD THROUGH LONGSUFFERING

We can bear up under almost anything if we have hope and if we know that we are loved.

Think of the ups and downs of God's chosen people. They began with Abraham, then Isaac, then Jacob. And from Jacob (Israel) came twelve sons which became the twelve tribes of Israel. They almost died of starvation due to a seven year famine. But God sent Jacob's one son Joseph ahead of them. He was rejected by his brothers, sold to slave traders, became a servant in an Egyptian household, was falsely accused of rape and sent to prison, and from there—in one day—God raised him to second in command of Egypt. From this position Joseph rescued his father and brothers and brought them to Egypt to live. In Egypt they were blessed and they multiplied. But over the years they became too large and powerful. The Egyptians became fearful of their power, so they made slaves of them.

But God had not forgotten them. God delivered his people out of 400 years of Egyptian slavery. It was a miraculous deliverance, including the parting of the Red Sea where they crossed over in safety, but the sea collapsed in on their enemy and destroyed them all. They crossed over a desert where there was no food or water, but God provided. Then they came to the land of promise. It was lush, just as God had promised them, but there was a concern. It was inhabited already, and they would have to fight to take it over. They were afraid of the challenge, so back to the dessert they went. Forty years later their children had grown up and God gave their children another chance. They believed God, and God gave them victory over all their enemies. God gave the victory, but they still had to fight.

After conquering the various nations and making them their own, they became lax and prideful. They took on the gods of other nations and lost sight of the God who loved them and provided for them. God gave them one chance after another to repent and return to him, but after about 300 years of this rebellion God removed their blessing. He sent the Babylonians into Jerusalem to take his people into captivity.

Even in captivity, God had not forgotten or rejected them. He even gave them prosperity there if they submitted to his will. **Think of the setbacks of this nation over the past thousand years**. Think of the lengthy suffering they endured. And now, after being in exile in Babylon for seventy years, God encouraged his people. He never forgot them, and he never stopped loving them. **He still had a plan for them**: He spoke to them with these words:

"For I know the plans I have for you," declares the LORD, **"plans to prosper you and not to harm you, plans to give you hope and a future**." Jeremiah 29:11

God's chosen people went through hundreds of years of intense suffering, but God was still in control. He continued to love them. And he had a prosperous plan for them. Suffering and setbacks are part of this life. It is not because God does not love us or because we have no future. It is because we live in a fallen world. We are fallen and the devil is fallen. Jesus referred to the devil as the "Prince of this World". He rules here on earth, and he rules through sinful, ignorant men. This all began when the serpent tempted Eve and called God a liar. Man was cast from this lush Garden at that point, and suffering and death set in. We suffer in this world because mankind chose to set out on his own, not because God has forgotten us. There is a day when we will be totally delivered from all this misery. That is our ultimate hope, not in the time at hand or in the things of this world.

Why are you downcast, O my soul? Why so disturbed within me? **Put your hope in God, for I will yet praise him, my Savior and my God**. Psalm 42:11

Just as God repeatedly delivered his people from bondage and gave them victory over all their enemies, he will deliver us if we come to him and submit to him. Sin is our bondage. Our sinful flesh, the devil and the world he leads are our enemies. There is no life in these. Life only comes from God, for God is life. If we seek God now, he will deliver us now from these enemies. **This must happen first if we also want his prosperity**. Look at Paul's words to Timothy about the importance of putting our hope in God— whether things are going well for us or not. In either situation, our hope in God alone is critical for true hope and future prosperity.

The widow who is really in need and left all alone **puts her hope in God** and continues night and day to pray and to ask God for help. But the widow who lives for pleasure is dead even while she lives.
1 Timothy 5:5-6

Command those who are rich in this present world not to be arrogant **nor to put their hope in wealth, which is so uncertain, but to put their hope in God, who richly provides us with everything for our enjoyment.** Command them to do good, to be rich in good deeds, and to be generous and willing to share. In this way they will lay up treasure for themselves as a firm foundation for the coming age, **so that they may take hold of the life that is truly life.** 1 Timothy 6:17-19

JESUS IS TRUE LIFE AND THE ONLY SOURCE

The only source of true life is Jesus. God is the creator of life. He is life. We seek life in all sorts of ways, but all we find is death. We look to drugs, money, prestige, power, people, status, possessions, personal strength, intelligence, reputation, etc. But all of these come up empty. Only God is good, and all good things come from him (Matthew 19:17, Genesis 1:31). All of mankind is seeking life—true life. But this true life only comes from God through Jesus.

Jesus answered, "**I am the way and the truth and the life.** No one comes to the Father except through me. John 14:6

For God so loved the world that he gave his one and only Son, that whoever believes in him shall not perish **but have eternal life**. John 3:16

Jesus gives his own Spirit freely to all who come to him. His Spirit is a well of life that flows from within each person that receives him. This is the only true source of life.

If anyone is thirsty, let him come to me and drink. Whoever believes in me, as the Scripture has said, streams of living water will flow from within him." By this he meant the Spirit, whom those who believed in him were later to receive. Up to that time the Spirit had not been given, since Jesus had not yet been glorified. John 7:37-39

The Spirit and the bride say, "Come!" And let him who hears say, "Come!" Whoever is thirsty, let him come; and whoever wishes, let him take **the free gift of the water of life**. Revelation 22:17

Our only true hope is in God because he is the only true source of life. For many of us our frustrations over our lives comes from searching in all the wrong places. Hope requires faith in God's love for us. If we do not believe God for his love and blessings for us, we will not seek him. The reality is that God longs for us to seek him in faith. He longs to bless us as his dearly loved children. God is love, and he loves us beyond measure. He desires for us to seek him for his blessings.

And without faith it is impossible to please God, because anyone who comes to him must believe that he exists and that **he rewards those who earnestly seek him**. Hebrews 11:6

It's a trade—our life for his. Our life is dying, weak, wounded and misled. His life is eternal. It is the only life that fulfills. There is no value that can be put upon it, for the worth is infinite. Jesus longs to make the trade. We give up our decrepit, dying life for his eternal life. It is a fantastic deal, but we have to make the choice to give this life up to him. We cannot hold onto both lives; they are incompatible with each other. It's our choice to make, a choice between life and death. (Matthew 7:24-27)

GOD HAS A GOOD FUTURE AND PURPOSE FOR US

This life can be very difficult for sure. Many of us go through life with suffering and loss. There are any number of ways that our lives can become rattled: divorce, sickness, death, injury, loss of job, loss of a loved one, rejection, loss of possessions, etc. In these hard times it is a battle against discouragement and depression. But we must always realize that we live in a fallen world that is led by a fallen angelic creature, the devil. Jesus called him the "prince of this world". We also battle against our own fallen nature, and we live in a society where everyone was born with a fallen nature. Death and suffering were not the intent for God's creation; they are the result of rebellion against God. God warned Adam, the first man created, that he should not eat of the tree in the middle of the garden, the tree of the knowledge of good and evil. God warned that if man ate of this tree he would die. But man was deceived by the devil and he believed the devil's lies and ate of this tree anyway. As a result, we have all tasted death and destruction in our lives.

However, the story does not end there. God still loves us. He created us to have a good life, full of purpose and meaning. However, the only truly good purpose and meaning is according to God's nature and God's plan for our lives. He knows the place that we are in and that it is miserable. He understands our wounds and pains. He feels for us. He desires to redeem us from our pits and to raise us up with him.

Praise the LORD, O my soul; all my inmost being, praise his holy name. Praise the LORD, O my soul, and **forget not all his benefits—who forgives all your sins and heals all your diseases, who redeems your life from the pit and crowns you with love and compassion, who satisfies your desires with good things so that your youth is renewed like the eagle's**. Psalm 103:1-5

Now, we are all in the same place that Adam and Eve were in at the beginning. Will we believe God at his word, or will we trust in a lie from the devil, his world, our sinful flesh and our view of the world around us? God's Word is filled with promises of life if we choose to follow his ways and trust him with our lives. But the choice is ours. The promise that he gave his people of long ago still holds for us.

This day I call heaven and earth as witnesses against you that I have set before you life and death, blessings and curses. **Now choose life**, so that you and your children may live and that you may love the LORD your God, listen to his voice, and hold fast to him. For **the LORD is your life**, and he will give you many years in the land he swore to give to your fathers, Abraham, Isaac and Jacob. Deuteronomy 30:19-20

We have the choice of life and death, and God is our life—if we so choose him. If we do not choose him, we have already made the choice for death.

We may be one of billions of people on the earth, but each one of us is unique, and each one of us is known by God. He knows your name. He personally knows the details of your life. And for each one of us, he has a special purpose for which we were created. We all struggle to have purpose in life, but we struggle looking in all the wrong places. It is God's purposes that must prevail for us to find fulfillment in life. We all need to be seeking him for the direction of our lives. It is God who establishes his work for us.

The LORD will fulfill his purpose for me; your love, O LORD, endures forever—do not abandon the works of your hands. Psalm 138:8

Our lives on earth are temporary. All of us should be living our lives so that we store up treasures in heaven. This can be done in any situation of life—in loss or gain, in riches or poverty, in prison or free, in worldly failure or worldly prosperity. God's promises are for everyone who believes and has faith in God's Word and his love for them.

WHO IS IN CONTROL OF OUR FUTURE?

We all need to look beyond this present life and look far into eternity. It is like storing up our 401K for retirement, except, this retirement is God's eternal rest in his kingdom. In order to do this we have to make a choice. If we store up for this life, we will spend ourselves on the things of this life and miss our eternal resting place. (Luke 23:39-43, 1 Corinthians 15:19)

"Do not store up for yourselves treasures on earth, where moth and rust destroy, and where thieves break in and steal. But **store up for yourselves treasures in heaven**, where moth and rust do not destroy, and where thieves do not break in and steal. For where your treasure is, there your heart will be also. Matthew 6:19-21

Jesus gave these instructions about storing up treasures in heaven. And he also gave a promise for this life. He was talking about how people worry and fret about all of their worldly necessities: food, clothing shelter, etc. Men are constantly seeking security in this life. They use up all their energy seeking them. Jesus said that the pagans run after all these things. They use up all of their being seeking what God would provide for us just because he loves us—if only we would seek his kingdom and his righteousness.

For the pagans run after all these things, and **your heavenly Father knows that you need them**. But **seek first his kingdom and his righteousness**, and all these things will be given to you as well. Therefore do not worry about tomorrow, for tomorrow will worry about itself. Each day has enough trouble of its own. Matthew 6:32-34

God is in control of the past, present and the future. For us, we cannot undo the past, but God can redeem it and heal our wounds. We try to plan the future, but tomorrow belongs to the Lord, and he will put all things into place as he pleases. All we have is today, and even for today, we are fully dependent upon God who is in control of the past, present and the future.

God is in control of all things. We only think that we are in control. Most of our lacking in this world is because we set our hearts on the things of this world and we do not set our hearts on the things of God's kingdom. The only way to truly be in control is to believe God's commands and promises for us and to walk in them, trusting that God will come through on his word. If we are angry with ourselves and our lives, we ought to be angry that we do not seek and trust God. The direction we take in life is dependent upon whether we believe that God cares for us and that he will lift up our lives if we humble ourselves under his loving might.

Humble yourselves, therefore, under God's mighty hand, that **he may lift you up** in due time. Cast all your anxiety on him because **he cares for you**. 1 Peter 5:6-7

We have an infinitely marvelous future in Christ Jesus. But we cannot see it if we constantly focus on the terrible past, how bad today is, and the fear of our dismal tomorrow. This thinking comes from depending upon others, the things of this world and ourselves for the blessings of life.

Since, then, **you have been raised with Christ, set your hearts on things above, where Christ is seated at the right hand of God. Set your minds on things above, not on earthly things.** For you died, and

your life is now hidden with Christ in God. When **Christ, who is your life,** appears, then **you also will appear with him in glory**.
Colossians 3:1-4

True riches and blessings only come from God, and all we have to do to receive them is to have faith in God, to seek him and trust him for his life to be poured out on us, in us and through us. He is a God who loves us and desires to bless his children with good things. He desires to protect them and lead them as they walk through life. God is not absent in our relationship with him. Faith is really our relationship that we pursue with God. Our relationship with our loving Creator is waiting upon our faith. God is waiting and ready.

And without faith it is impossible to please God, because anyone who comes to him **must believe that he exists and that he rewards those who earnestly seek him**. Hebrews 11:6

We hopelessly look at our life, and in our despair we seek out more and more of what the world has to provide for us, thinking that if we have what the world provides we will be happy. But it never satisfies, and we become more disheartened and angry with life and ourselves. But Jesus warned us about setting our hearts on such foolishness.

"Watch out! Be on your guard against all kinds of greed; **a man's life does not consist in the abundance of his possessions.**" Luke 12:15

Jesus talked about a man who stored up more and more riches in this life, thinking that he was now secure. God called this man a fool. The man had not considered his short life on this earth. He had not planned for his eternal future. And Jesus said,

"This is how it will be with anyone who stores up things for himself but is **not rich toward God**." Luke 12:21

Anyone who is angry and depressed about his life is looking at his control over his life, which is nil. He is also looking at the life that this fallen world provides, which is no life at all. This world and this life are passing away, so only a fool would put his hopes in them. No, our hope is in the life God has for us, and it does not end with the few years we have here. Jesus told us to store up treasures in heaven, but we will store up treasures wherever we have put our hearts. If our hearts are on the things of this life, we will be disappointed. If our hearts are on things above, our hope will sustain us and we will not be disappointed. Jesus also said,

For where your treasure is, there your heart will be also. Luke 12:34

Read all of Luke 12:14-34.

GOD HAS A PURPOSE IN HIS KINGDOM NOW

We live in a fallen world that is ruled by the devil, "the prince of this world". We are aliens in a foreign land. This world in its present state is not our homeland. Furthermore, there is an intense battle raging in our midst. It is a battle between the kingdom of darkness and the kingdom of light. We should expect for there to be assaults of hardship—physical, mental and emotional hardships. We all should be fighting the battle for the kingdom of light. Take the example of Apostle Paul. He did not have a pleasant life in this world. Look at his description of his life as he fought for Jesus' kingdom.

I have worked much harder, been in prison more frequently, been flogged more severely, and been exposed to death again and again. Five times I received from the Jews the forty lashes minus one. Three times I was beaten with rods, once I was stoned, three times I was shipwrecked, I spent a night and a day in the open sea, I have been constantly on the move. I have been in danger from rivers, in danger from bandits, in danger from my own countrymen, in danger from Gentiles; in danger in the city, in danger in the country, in danger at sea; and in danger from false brothers. I have labored and toiled and have often gone without sleep; I have known hunger and thirst and have often gone without food; I have been cold and naked. Besides everything else, I face daily the pressure of my concern for all the churches. Who is weak, and I do not feel weak? Who is led into sin, and I do not inwardly burn? 2 Corinthians 11:23-29

Paul was not discouraged and hopeless because of his many hardships. On the contrary! He knew that his hope was in the day when he would return to his homeland in the Kingdom of God, victorious in his battles of this life. God loves us in our struggles, and he has work for us to do in the midst of our struggles. Look again at Paul. In addition to the hardships listed above, he spent years in prison for his faith in Jesus. He was not discouraged. Instead, he saw that his life was being used by his Creator, and he joyfully worked for his Creator in the midst of his imprisonment. Look at part of his letter that he wrote to the church in Philippi from his prison cell.

Now I want you to know, brothers, that what has happened to me has really served to advance the gospel. As a result, it has become clear throughout the whole palace guard and to everyone else that I am in chains for Christ. Because of my chains, most of the brothers in the Lord have been encouraged to speak the word of God more courageously and fearlessly. Philippians 1:12-14

We are aliens and strangers on this earth. We need to live each day with this realization and attitude. We live in a fallen world. Our suffering is a consequence of this fallen world and life. If we suffer, it is not because God has forgotten us or does not love us. Rather, it is because this is not our final destiny. We must press on, endure and constantly look to our Lord for his presence and guidance and strength. Look at what some of our predecessors went through.

Some faced jeers and flogging, while still others were chained and put in prison. They were stoned; they were sawed in two; they were put to death by the sword. They went about in sheepskins and goatskins, destitute, persecuted and mistreated—the world was not worthy of them. They wandered in deserts and mountains, and in caves and holes in the ground. Hebrews 11:36-38

How did they withstand these hardships without breaking? They had hope in the future God prepared for them.

All these people were still living by faith when they died. They did not receive the things promised; they only saw them and welcomed them from a distance. And **they admitted that they were aliens and strangers on earth**. People who say such things show that they are **looking for a country of their own**. If they had been thinking of the country they had left, they would have had opportunity to return. Instead, **they were longing for a better country—a heavenly one**. Therefore God is not ashamed to be called their God, for he has prepared a city for them. Hebrews 11:13-16

Job suffered severely. He was a faithful man who had a prosperous relationship with God. God gave him good health, a large family, many possessions and a very pleasant happy life. But one day God allowed Satan to take it all away from Job—and Job was not aware of the work of Satan. All Job knew was that his life was being sapped from him.

God allowed Job's property, wealth, business, children and health to be taken. Job was being used by God as a witness to Satan to show his faithfulness to God in the face of having his blessings removed. Job was unaware of Satan's hand in all this. Job remained faithful, and when the test was complete, God restored Job's wealth to an even greater measure. (Job 42:10-16)

Before:		After:
Sons	7	7
Daughters	3	3
Sheep	7,000	14,000
Camels	3,000	6,000
Oxen	500	1,000
Donkeys	500	1,000

This is a nice teaching, but unless we focus on God, his specific purposes for each of us, and how he might use us, we will remain in a hopeless situation. We must focus on two aspects of our future—our future on this earth and our eternal future in the kingdom of God. God has a purpose for each one of us in his kingdom now in this present life. We need to be seeking God, asking him to reveal and fulfill his purposes through our lives. Then we need to be obedient and walk in his callings in our lives. If we shrink back into our worldly life, we will never see his fulfillment for us.

It is never too late, and it is never impossible. The real question, are we willing to endure the cost of serving God. There will be a cost, but the benefit will be a life with purpose—God's purposes.

Reflection question

How can God use you here today in your present situation? Where can you work to bear fruit for him in the specific aspects of your present life?

Chapter Nine

Temper Tantrums and Pity Parties

Up until now we have been dealing with anger that is driven by unforgiveness or a wounded heart. In this lesson and the next three lessons we will delve into anger caused by our own selfish sinful nature.

Those of us who have raised children have all seen temper tantrums. Little two year old Johnny does not get his way, so he screams and cries. He kicks and slams doors. He lies on the floor kicking his feet and throwing a fit, expecting others to give in to his will. His behavior is two fold. He wants those in authority to give in to him, and he also wants them to feel like they have done wrong. He makes himself out to be a victim.

It is a good thing that we grow out of temper tantrums—or do we? Or do we just grow out of the old way and develop adult temper tantrums? We would feel foolishly embarrassed if we laid on the floor kicking and screaming as an adult. But if our hearts have not changed, maybe we still have temper tantrums where we demand our selfish ways and project ourselves as the victim when things do not go our way. Our angry behavior may just be a childish temper tantrum. Our pouting and sulking may be totally self-focused with the heart motive to manipulate the response of others.

What controls our actions? We all have a complex nature, and a battle goes on inside of us. Our sinful flesh insists on being the master. Think of smoking. Most people who smoke want to quit. It is costly, unhealthy and smelly. So why don't smokers just stop smoking? It is because the flesh rules over the desires of the mind. You may want to quit, but the flesh gets its way. What about losing weight. People who are a hundred pounds or more overweight did not decide to be fat, and they do not want to be fat. So why don't they just lose weight. All they have to do is eat less, eat right and exercise more. Again, the flesh says "EAT", and the will of the mind gives into the flesh.

Emotions are another major driver to our actions. The mind of a man is to rule over the desires of our emotions. It is not that we should not have emotions. God has emotions, and we were created to be like him. Without emotions we would be lifeless robots. The key is not to stuff or deny emotions. The key is that our emotions should not rule over the mind. For example, the sex drive is good and should be reserved for marriage. The strong drive to look at pornography should be denied by the decisions of the mind. It is sin, and if the flesh gets its way it will likely mean a destroyed marriage and family.

Anger is no different. We have become accustomed to allowing the rage of anger within us to reign. James wrote that we should be "slow to become angry, for man's anger does not bring about the righteous life that God desires". (James 1:19-20) Paul instructs us to "get rid" of anger, rage, brawling, bitterness, malice, slander and filthy language. (Ephesians 4:31, Colossians 3:8) In other words, these men are telling us that we need to have control over the emotions of anger that attempt to reign over us. We are to rule over our emotions. Our emotions should not be allowed to rule over us. When anger begins, we need to rebuke it. We are to deny its power to stir up within us and drive us into actions that are purely selfish in nature—a temper tantrum. We allow anger to rage because we expect to manipulate and force others to comply with our selfish will.

We all need to be consciously aware of the battles that go on within us and to consciously take dominion over our flesh that wants to rule our actions. If given a million dollars to control our anger for a month, most of us could control our urge to become angry. We do not lack capability; we lack the will to be in control.

When Jesus was baptized and the Holy Spirit came upon him, the first thing the Spirit did was to lead him into the desert to fast for forty days and be tempted by the devil. (Matthew 4:1-11) Jesus was not without temptation. (Hebrews 4:15) But he had dominion over his flesh. Like Jesus, we are to put to death the misdeeds of the fleshly nature and live in the control, power and leading of the Holy Spirit. (Romans 8:12-14)

We have all inherited a sinful nature, going all the way back to the first sin of Adam and Eve. Our sinful nature drives us to look at ourselves as being the center of life. God is the center of all of life, but we struggle with that truth. Our nature tells us a lie that we are the center, and that we should rise up and care for ourselves first. When things do not go the way we wanted them, we get angry. In the end anger does not bless us. Anger can have serious consequences. Let's look at an angry incident between Adam and Eve's first two sons. (Now read Genesis 4:2-12.)

Then the LORD said to Cain, "**Why are you angry?** Why is your face downcast? If you do what is right, will you not be accepted? But if you do not do what is right, **sin is crouching at your door; it desires to have you, but you must master it.**" Genesis 4:6-7

Cain's anger led him to kill his brother, and as a result, God drove him to a distant land. Our self driven anger has the capacity to destroy our lives and to drive us far from God.

Our sinful anger can bring about great destruction in our lives and the lives of others. There may be times when our anger is righteously motivated, but most of the time it is born out of our selfish sinful nature.

Anger in itself is not necessarily sin, but it can be the result of our own sinful nature, or we may sin out of our anger. Let's give a definition of anger:

105

Anger is our emotional response to an unmet expectation.

For example, I expected that my son would have cut the grass while I was at work, as he was told. When I came home, I found that the grass had not been cut and my son is off with his friends. I blowup, take it out on my wife, threaten to ground my lazy son for a month, and then proceed to cut the grass myself—full steam ahead. My unmet expectation caused all this grief on my wife, my son and on me. I am having a temper tantrum over my unmet expectation.

We all have unmet expectations, but how do we handle our unmet expectations? Do we worry and fret? Do we get over anxious? Do we take our ill feelings out on others? Do we sin in our anger?

The feelings of anger are not necessarily sin, but they can drive us to sin. Sin is always against someone. It may be against ourselves. It may be against someone else. It is always against God. Our nature drives us toward sin, so we must oppose it. God instructs us to control our anger and to be silent while we search out our hearts to understand what is so upsetting.

> **In your anger do not sin**; when you are on your beds, search your hearts and be silent. Psalm 4:4

Anger may not be sinful. We may even be justified to be angry. But in order to walk righteously, our anger must not control us. We must be in control of it.

> My dear brothers, take note of this: Everyone should be quick to listen, slow to speak and **slow to become angry, for man's anger does not bring about the righteous life that God desires.** Therefore, get rid of all moral filth and the evil that is so prevalent and humbly accept the word planted in you, which can save you. James 1:19-21 (Psalm 37:8)

106

Forgiveness can stop a fight. Sin can start one. Don't fall prey to the devil's schemes. Do not stew over your anger day after day. Settle it before the day ends.

> **"In your anger do not sin": Do not let the sun go down while you are still angry, and do not give the devil a foothold.**
> Ephesians 4:26-27

Most of our anger is resolved if we resolve to grow up and stop having temper tantrums.

A temper tantrum is any reaction on our part that says, "I must have my way!" Much of our anger is pure selfishness. It demands others to give in to me. It is self focused and controlling.

James testifies to this definition.

> What causes fights and quarrels among you? Don't they come from your desires that battle within you? You want something but don't get it. You kill and covet, but you cannot have what you want. You quarrel and fight. You do not have, because you do not ask God. When you ask, you do not receive, because you ask with wrong motives, that you may spend what you get on your pleasures.
> James 4:1-3

We have come to believe that anger is some sort of a disease that we have to submit to with little or no choice in the matter. In reality, we have every choice. The choice is to deny our right to become angry when our expectations are not met. A patient man is wise. An angry man is a fool.

Patience brings him honor. A quick temper brings him shame. It is a choice to become wise.

> **A fool gives full vent to his anger, but a wise man keeps himself under control.** Proverbs 29:11

It is a choice to be patient and understanding. It is a question of being under control. Does anger control you, or do you control your anger?

> **A patient man has great understanding**, but a quick-tempered man displays folly. Proverbs 14:29

We can choose to overlook an offense for the sake of peace. The man who chooses to be patient and forgiving is wise in the eyes of God.

> **A man's wisdom gives him patience; it is to his glory to overlook an offense.** Proverbs 19:11

Most offenses can be overlooked. Anger is commonly used to get our way, but true strength is not shown in our outward, demanding, angry behavior. There is much greater strength in patience!

> **Better a patient man than a warrior**, a man who controls his temper than one who takes a city. Proverbs 16:32

> **Through patience a ruler can be persuaded, and a gentle tongue can break a bone.** Proverbs 25:15

We get angry when we are not in control of the situation. We think that in our anger that everyone will come running to respond to our demands. This may work to some degree with our young children. But it won't work with most adults. Actually, it doesn't give the result we desire in our family either. Our hostile anger alienates our family members from us, and in the end our relationships are in harmful disarray. There is even more to become frustrated over as a consequence of our fits of rage. Not only are we angry, but we have incited everyone else, and now everyone is hurt and angry.

How much do we arouse other's anger with our critical, angry words? Do we get angry when attacked by their words of anger? The wise man will control himself and see the situation for what it is, an attack. We can choose not to enter into the battle. God empowers us by his Holy Spirit within us to have control over our anger and to become peaceful, patient and kind.

> But the **fruit of the Spirit** is love, joy, **peace, patience, kindness**, goodness, faithfulness, gentleness and self-control. Against such things there is no law. Galatians 5:22-23

Remember, God is love, and we were created in the image of God. Those who belong to God, those who have received his forgiveness and his Spirit, are commanded to love, to be selfless, to have control over their anger.

> **Love is patient, love is kind**. It does not envy, it does not boast, it is not proud. **It is not rude**, it is **not self-seeking, it is not easily angered, it keeps no record of wrongs**. Love does not delight in evil but rejoices with the truth. It always protects, always trusts, always hopes, always perseveres. **Love never fails**.
> 1 Corinthians 13:4-8

We are commanded to get rid of our bitterness, rage and anger. We are commanded to be kind, compassionate and forgiving. This is a choice to be obedient to God and to become like God in his character.

> Do not let any unwholesome talk come out of your mouths, but only what is helpful for building others up according to their needs, that it

may benefit those who listen. And do not grieve the Holy Spirit of God, with whom you were sealed for the day of redemption. **Get rid of all bitterness, rage and anger**, brawling and slander, along with every form of malice. **Be kind and compassionate to one another, forgiving each other, just as in Christ God forgave you**. Ephesians 4:29-32

But now **you must rid yourselves of all such things as these: anger, rage**, malice, slander, and filthy language from your lips. Do not lie to each other, since **you have taken off your old self with its practices and have put on the new self, which is being renewed in knowledge in the image of its Creator.** Colossians 3:8-10

Temper tantrums and pity-parties (pouting) are a consequence of our sinful nature. We did not have to be taught how to have them; they come naturally from birth. Little kids do not have to be taught to lie on the floor, kick and scream and cry, hoping to get their way. These temper tantrums come naturally. Instead, our children need to be trained through discipline to be self-controlled and to restrain from temper tantrums. We are to crucify the sinful nature and to live for Christ.

We may chuckle about how our children might act, but we adults throw adult temper tantrums and pity parties. Let's define a few terms:

Temper tantrum: An act of anger to manipulate and intimidate. We are born with these capabilities, like pooping our pants. It's just as messy and smelly!!!

Pity party: Sulking in order to proclaim how badly hurt we are in order to blame and manipulate others. A victim mentality.

How often do a husband and wife go to bed angry and hurt? They lie there with their backs to each other, silent, stewing and unable to sleep. We give each other the silent treatment, expecting the other to break down and say something. We expect them to respond to our "silent hurt" as we have our pity party. Then, if the silence is broken, we accuse and blame and sulk.

Jesus, who is God, did not have temper tantrums or pity-parties when his created beings rebelled against him like little selfish brats. Instead, he bore our sins.

> When they hurled their insults at him, he did not retaliate; when he suffered, he made no threats. Instead, he entrusted himself to him who judges justly. He himself bore our sins in his body on the tree, so that we might die to sins and live for righteousness; by his wounds you have been healed. 1 Peter 2:23-24

We are to be like Jesus!

Reflection questions

How do you demand, intimidate, or manipulate others in order to get your way?

What is your reaction when you don't get your way? How are you stubborn?

How much of your anger is a temper tantrum?
A pity party? In other words, how much do you use your anger to get your way?

Chapter Ten

The Hot Temper

This lesson is an extension of the previous lesson on temper tantrums and pity parties. A hot temper may be driven by the spoiled fleshly nature. Or, it may be driven by a wounded and/or bitter heart that is filled with judgments. In either case, with the hot-temper, the outward behavior is much more harmful and extreme.

A hot-temper is an extreme temper tantrum. It is selfish and breeds upon man's own selfish desires with no concern or love for others. The hot-temper gets us in trouble. <u>The aim of a hot temper is to hurt someone, either physically or emotionally.</u> Physical displays of anger, hitting, grabbing, shoving, pounding, breaking things, shouting, cursing, threatening, commanding, hurtful words; these are all from a hot temper.

There are many consequences following the hot temper.

A **hot-tempered man must pay the penalty**; if you rescue him, you will have to do it again. Proverbs 19:19

He alienates most of his relationships. He wounds those around him—their hearts and possibly their bodies. His hot temper ruins his own life.

Since a hot temper is an out of control temper, he may do unlawful material and bodily damage. The penalty could lead to imprisonment. It is difficult to counsel him out of his hot temper because he is usually stubborn and does not listen to wise counsel. And like the proverb says, you can rescue him, but he will repeat his violent temper tantrum all over again and again. His whole life is driven by and characterized by his hot temper.

A hot-tempered man is impatient, and his highest priority is getting his own way or venting his anger. His selfish motives come before relationships, which he readily destroys.

A hot-tempered man stirs up dissension, but a **patient man calms a quarrel**. Proverbs 15:18

Not only does he ruin his relationships. Those who know his hot temper are wise to stay away from him. His anger can arouse the anger of others because of his harsh offensive nature. It spreads—maybe to you. Stay away from very angry people.

Do not make friends with a hot-tempered man, do not associate with one easily angered, or you may learn his ways and get yourself ensnared. Proverbs 22:24-25

We have said that anger is not necessarily sin, but that we are not to sin out of our anger. The hot tempered man always sins out of his anger. He sins against his loved ones and against himself. No one wants to be around him because of his offensive temper.

An angry man stirs up dissension, and a hot-tempered one commits many sins. Proverbs 29:22

In spite of the sin, most hot tempered people need our compassion. More than likely they were abused as a child. They are frustrated with life,

114

and even though their actions are sinful, they are wounded on the inside. A hot temper is usually linked to a wounded heart and/or a frustrated life. Frustration comes from being out of control when life is being severely challenged. If you have a hot temper, what should you do about it?

Action:

- Confess and repent (Join with an accountability partner.) "If we confess our sins, he is faithful and just and will forgive us our sins and purify us from all unrighteousness." 1 John 1:9 It is God who will forgive us and purify our hearts from the roots of our anger— assuming we confess our sin to him and to fellow Christians. If we remain in hiding, we cannot expect deliverance or life or even forgiveness.

- Pray! Go to the only one who does spiritual heart surgery on your spiritual heart. "The LORD your God will circumcise your hearts and the hearts of your descendants, so that you may love him with all your heart and with all your soul, and live." Deuteronomy 30:6

- Apologize and ask for forgiveness from those you offended. Your anger has wounded the hearts of those who are closest to you. You are destroying yourself, and all those around you. Humbly go to them, asking for forgiveness with the hope of mending the relationships.

- Continually examine your deeper roots. It is good to control your rages, but it is even better to remove the roots of the anger. In fact, if you don't remove the roots, they will sprout their ugly heads again.

- Go to the Lord with your frustrations and anxieties. Much of our anxiety is a result of taking on burdens that we are incapable of carrying. In truth, we are all very weak beings. We like to think of ourselves as independent and strong. But we are all very weak and totally dependant upon God for provision, wisdom, protection, direction, strength, etc. Psalm 94:18-19, 1 Peter 5:6-10; Philippians 4:6-7

Reflections questions

Be honest with yourself and with your group.

Are others afraid of you or intimidated by you? Your friends? Your wife? Your children?

Are you easily upset or offended?

Does your anger flare up in a rage?

How do you express your anger? Physically? Verbally?

What frustrations are you experiencing that arouse your anger?

Chapter Eleven

Grumbling and Complaining

(Fault finding, blaming and belittling the ones we have anger against.)

Grumbling and complaining is common to all of us. Normally we feel justified to complain and gripe. After all, aren't we the ones who have been cheated and abused by others? We are the victim! Why should we be blamed for verbalizing what others have done to us? But if we could see the true motives of our hearts, we would have a different viewpoint. The Bible speaks very strongly about grumbling and complaining. It is much more serious than most of us think.

Grumbling and complaining is a form of anger. It may not be violent or hot-tempered, but it can be driven by the same selfish motivation. We are commanded not to argue or complain so that we can become blameless and pure.

Do everything without complaining or arguing, so that you may become blameless and pure, children of God without fault in a crooked and depraved generation, in which you shine like stars in the universe... Philippians 2:14-15

<u>**Grumbling and complaining is the opposite of thankfulness. It is**</u>
<u>**forever looking at life and proclaiming that all is bad and that we have**</u>
<u>**been cheated and abused by someone. In essence we say, "You don't**</u>
<u>**love me!"**</u>

<u>**Grumbling and complaining is rebellion against God.**</u> This picture is
clearly seen from a study of the Israelites.

God's people, the Israelites, had grown to a great number in Egypt. The
Egyptians had become fearful of their powerful numbers, so they subjected
them to harsh slavery. They had been in this bondage for 400 years when
God sent Moses to deliver them from their suffering. God sent ten
miraculous plaques before Pharaoh finally let them go. But as they left,
Pharaoh had a change of heart and sent his armies after them. Again God
delivered them by parting the Red Sea so his people could cross over on dry
land, but then he allowed the water to come crashing down on the Egyptian
army who was in pursuit.

Then God led them across the dessert to a lush land that he had
promised to give them. When they got there they sent twelve men to spy
out the land. They came back with glowing reports about how it was
everything that God had promised. However, it was already inhabited. God
promised to deliver the land into their hands, but ten of the twelve spies
were afraid and recommended that they not go in. They did not believe God
would bring them victory, even though they had just witnessed such a great
deliverance from Egyptian bondage. God sent them back out into the
dessert for forty years until the rebellious generation died off.

That is a brief summary of the account. Now let's look deeper into the
Scriptures to see the nature of their grumbling and complaining.

The Israelites had just seen God's powerful hand with the ten plaques
and the parting of the Red Sea. They had traveled just three days into the
dessert when they began to grumble and complain.

> Then Moses led Israel from the Red Sea and they went into the
> Desert of Shur. For three days they traveled in the desert without
> finding water. When they came to Marah, they could not drink its water

118

because it was bitter. (That is why the place is called Marah.) **So the people grumbled against Moses, saying, "What are we to drink?"**

Then Moses cried out to the LORD, and the LORD showed him a piece of wood. He threw it into the water, and the water became sweet. Exodus 15:22-25

Grumbling and complaining is a grievous sin. The Israelites wandered in the desert for forty years and lost their opportunity to enter the Promised Land because of their rebellious grumbling and complaining. We are warned today not to fall as they did. (Hebrews 3:7-4:11) The following verses should be read before class by each student for a clear picture of grumbling and complaining: [Exodus 15:24-17:3, Numbers 14:1-36, 16:11, 16:41 17:5, 17:10, Deut. 1:27, Psalm 78, Psalm 106:25, James 5:9, Jude 16, Romans 13:1-7, 1 Corinthians 10:10]

The Israelites overflowed with complaints:

No Food: They had only been out of Egypt one and a half months, and they were ready to go back into bondage. [Read Exodus 16:1-16.] Instead of being thankful for their freedom, they complained about not having any food. They did not trust that God loved them and would feed them. Notice that they grumbled and complained against Moses and Aaron, but God heard their complaints and took them as against him. This should be a warning for us; that when we grumble and complain to others, about others or against others, we are really voicing our complaints against God who supplies all things.

The Israelites grumbled and complained about not having food, and God miraculously provided manna each day. This was an obvious miracle of provision from God. They complained about not having any meat, and God miraculously provided an enormous harvest of quail.

Now a wind went out from the LORD and drove quail in from the sea. It brought them down all around the camp to about **three feet above the ground, as far as a day's walk in any direction**. Numbers 11:31

No water: One would think that by this time they would stop their faithless grumbling and complaining and trust in God to provide whatever they needed. But that was not the case. They were in the desert and they became thirsty. Instead of seeking the Lord for water, they quarreled and complained to Moses again.

> The whole Israelite community set out from the Desert of Sin, traveling from place to place as the LORD commanded. They camped at Rephidim, but there was no water for the people to drink. So they **quarreled with Moses** and said, "Give us water to drink."
> Moses replied, **"Why do you quarrel with me? Why do you put the LORD to the test?"**
> But the people were thirsty for water there, and they **grumbled against Moses**. They said, "Why did you bring us up out of Egypt to make us and our children and livestock die of thirst?" Exodus 17:1-3

God was angry with their complaints and lack of faith in his love for them, but he provided water for them anyway. Moses struck a rock, and water gushed out.

Fear of enemies: The Lord brought his people across the desert to the land of promise. Twelve spies went in to check it out, and they came back with two reports. One, the land is everything that God promised. It was a lush and beautiful land, filled with vegetation. Two, it was also inhabited by large powerful people. If they wanted the land, they would have to fight for it. Again, one would think that by this time God would have sufficiently proven himself to these people. You would think they would have trusted in his protection, deliverance and provision. He faithfully demonstrated all three from his deliverance in Egypt and the crossing in the dessert. He

120

never let them down. But they continued to grumble and complain. They complained about food, and God fed them. They complained about water, and God provided water in the dessert. Now they were complaining about dying at the hands of their enemies.

They even accused God, saying that God brought them this far in order to destroy them by their enemies. They rejected Moses, the leader God provided, and devised to find a leader of their own choosing.

That night all the people of the community raised their voices and wept aloud. All the Israelites **grumbled against Moses and Aaron**, and the whole assembly said to them, "If only we had died in Egypt! Or in this desert! **Why is the LORD bringing us to this land only to let us fall by the sword?** Our wives and children will be taken as plunder. **Wouldn't it be better for us to go back to Egypt?**" And they said to each other, **"We should choose a leader and go back to Egypt."** Numbers 14:1-4

But you were unwilling to go up; you rebelled against the command of the LORD your God. **You grumbled in your tents and said, "The LORD hates us; so he brought us out of Egypt to deliver us into the hands of the Amorites to destroy us. Where can we go?** Our brothers have made us lose heart. They say, 'The people are stronger and taller than we are; the cities are large, with walls up to the sky. We even saw the Anakites there.'" Deuteronomy 1:26-28

These were a rebellious people, not trusting in God's love for them. They were not thankful for anything that God had done for them. Rather, they grumbled and complained about every aspect of their situation. They had completely forgotten how God delivered them from their bondage in Egypt, how God provided food and water in the desert. And now they had forgotten how God promised to them a fruitful land of their own that was already inhabited. (Exodus 3:17) They did not believe God or trust in his love for them—so they grumbled and complained.

Against Moses and Aaron: God had blessed his people by giving them two anointed leaders. God had demonstrated their anointing in Egypt through the ten plagues and the parting of the Red Sea. But whenever anything happened that the Israelites did not like, they harshly complained to and about their leaders. Moses had told them that the earth would open up and swallow all who opposed their leadership as a witness that they had been chosen by God. Even after this actually came true as the earth swallowed up 250 men before their eyes, they still complained about Moses and Aaron's leadership (Numbers 16:28-41).

> The next day the whole Israelite community **grumbled** against Moses and Aaron. "You have killed the LORD'S people," they said.
> Numbers 16:41

How often do we grumble and complain about the leaders placed over us? We complain about our boss, our president, governor, representatives, judges, parents, spouses, etc.

This is not to say that our leaders are perfect. On the contrary, our leaders are fallen from perfection just as we are. One aspect of that fall is our dishonor of those in authority. The Israelites did not honor Moses, who was chosen by God to rule over them. We must all come to realize that all authority comes from God and it is God who appoints leaders, and it is God who bestows authority upon them. Any complaint against them is a complaint against God.

> Everyone must submit himself to the governing authorities, for there is no authority except that which God has established. The authorities that exist have been established by God. Consequently, he who rebels against the authority is rebelling against what God has instituted, and those who do so will bring judgment on themselves. Romans 13:1-2

Against God: Actually, all grumbling and complaining is ultimately against God. It is God who is our provider and protector. It is his steps that we walk in. He is the one who determines our place in life. He is the one who puts parents, government leaders, bosses, etc. over us.   It is his authority that controls our lives. When we complain against any of these, we are ultimately complaining to God about the life he has given to us.

The Israelites did not see their complaints as against God, but against Moses and Aaron. But that is not how God saw it.

So Moses and Aaron said to all the Israelites, "In the evening you will know that it was the LORD who brought you out of Egypt, and in the morning you will see the glory of the LORD, because **he has heard your grumbling against him**. **Who are we, that you should grumble against us?**" Moses also said, "You will know that it was the LORD when he gives you meat to eat in the evening and all the bread you want in the morning, because **he has heard your grumbling against him**. **Who are we? You are not grumbling against us, but against the LORD.**"

Then Moses told Aaron, "Say to the entire Israelite community, 'Come before the LORD, for **he has heard your grumbling.**'"

While Aaron was speaking to the whole Israelite community, they looked toward the desert, and there was the glory of the LORD appearing in the cloud.

The LORD said to Moses, "**I have heard the grumbling of the Israelites.** Tell them, 'At twilight you will eat meat, and in the morning you will be filled with bread. Then you will know that I am the LORD your God.'" Exodus 16:6-12

THANKFULNESS—THE OPPOSITE OF COMPLAINING

The opposite of grumbling and complaining is thankfulness. The antidote to grumbling and complaining is thankfulness. We should be thankful to those around us, but just as complaining about our earthly leaders and providers is a complaint directly to God; thankfulness for anything upon this earth is thankfulness to God who provides those blessings. It is good to thank those who God uses to bless us, but it is more important to recognize that God—who is love, who loves us—is the one who is blessing us through others.

Caution: Hypocritical thanksgiving does not fool God. A hypocrite is someone who says one thing, but does another. If you grumble and complain about your job all day, and then thank God for providing for your material welfare at the dinner table, are you not a hypocrite? If you complain about your government in your circle of friends, and then thank God for living in this free country, are you not a hypocrite? If you complain and speak evil about your spouse to others, and then tell her you love her, are you not a hypocrite?

Anger is from the heart. Grumbling and complaining are from the heart. True thankfulness is from the heart. We are commanded to always be joyful, to pray at all times and to be thankful no matter what our circumstances.

Be joyful always; **pray continually**; **give thanks in all circumstances**, for this is God's will for you in Christ Jesus. 1 Thessalonians 5:16-18

God does not bless us one day and curse us the next. He does not hear our prayers one day and ignore us the next. He is always attentive to the prayers of his people, so we can thank him each and every day in every circumstance. He is there with us in our deepest struggles and our most restful pleasures. Contentment is a sign of being truly thankful and truly trusting God with the life he has given us. Contentment is a sign that we have given our lives to God and trust in his loving provision for us.

I am not saying this because I am in need, for **I have learned to be content whatever the circumstances**. I know what it is to be in need, and I know what it is to have plenty. **I have learned the secret of being**

124

content in any and every situation, whether well fed or hungry, whether living in plenty or in want. **I can do everything through him who gives me strength.** Philippians 4:11-13

We all need to repent of our grumbling and complaining and to worship God by focusing on all that he has done for us and all the ways he has blessed us. Thankfulness is the true antidote for our grumbling and complaining. If we grumble and complain to others, we are doing it unto God. In like manner, our thankfulness is an attitude about God's love for us. It is shown when we thank others as well as when we thank God directly. If we walk in thankfulness, our angry disposition will subside.

This is a spiritual battle. **"As thanks is to God, so complaining is to the devil."**

Disciplines:
- Set aside time each day to meditate on your blessings. Confess your blessings to God and express your appreciation and thankfulness.
- Imagine the effects on others (friends, family, supervisor, fellow workers). Become a blessing to others with your appreciative and joyful attitude about your life and your situations—all of them, easy or difficult.

Reflection questions

How many times a day do you complain?

How many times a day do you thank God for his blessings to you?

Do you blame or complain about others? Your boss? Fellow workers? Family and friends? Government officials? Anyone in authority?

If you were thankful in all things, what would make you angry?

Chapter Twelve

Quarreling

Anger frequently brews from a difference in opinion. Life is filled with disagreements. Sometimes we are right, and sometimes we are wrong. Quarrels arise when we have to be acknowledged as the one who is right—the one who gets his way, and not others.

Let's begin by defining a couple terms.

Argument: When two people are discussing a disagreement, and at least one is <u>not</u> listening, or one side is intent on making the other side wrong.

Reason together: Both are seeking to see the views of the other side, as well as revealing their own views.

It is good to express our opinions and to discuss each others views for the benefit of understanding on both sides. It is essential to discuss our views if we are ever to become like minded as the Bible commands us (Philippians 2:2) . A discussion or peaceful debate among humble people will bring about understanding and unity. But an argument will bring about a quarrel. The Proverbs are filled with wisdom regarding quarrels.

A hot-tempered man stirs up dissension, but **a patient man calms a quarrel**. Proverbs 15:18

In other words, be slow to react to defend your view. Notice that a hot-tempered man is the one who stirs up the quarrel and the dissension that results.

Starting a quarrel is like breaching a dam; **so drop the matter before a dispute breaks out**. Proverbs 17:14

A dam may hold back millions of tons of water. As long as the dam is in place, all is peaceful. But if the dam gives way, an entire town can be wiped out by a raging flood. Starting a quarrel is like breaking a huge hole in a dam, causing unstoppable damage. At the first sign of a quarrel, those of us who are wise and self-controlled should drop the matter and do whatever is necessary to walk in peace. We could just hold onto our opinion without expressing it. We could listen intently and quietly. We could seek reconciliation by expressing how much the relationship means to you and apologize for the friction and division. Or we could peacefully walk away. A quarrel stores up potential anger and fighting that can burst forth and foster an angry feud, so don't store up. Back off if an offense is brewing.

Most of us see quarreling as defending our rights. We may even see it as a righteous action of standing up for what we see as right. But some seek to have a quarrel. Seeking a quarrel is sin.

He who loves a quarrel loves sin; he who builds a high gate invites destruction. Proverbs 17:19

Like any sin, when we recognize it in ourselves, our obligation is to repent of it and walk in the other direction. The other direction is peace; we need to be peacemakers, not quarrelers. Jesus said,

128

Blessed are the peacemakers, for they will be called sons of God. Matthew 5:9

It is a choice. Do we want to be a quarrelsome, sinful fool, or do we want to be sons of God who seek peace?

We all need friends in this life. Quarreling ruins friendships. Even a fool needs friends, but a fool can ruin his relationships because of his selfish drive to argue. Out of his insecurity, he has to be right. He is a perpetual annoyance, and people will avoid him like a stench.

A foolish son is his father's ruin, and **a quarrelsome wife is like a constant dripping**. Proverbs 19:13

Nobody likes quarrelling. If you want friends, don't quarrel! Again, it is a choice. Do we want to be honored or classified as a troublesome fool?

It is to a man's honor to avoid strife, but **every fool is quick to quarrel**. Proverbs 20:3

Fools ruin relationships by quarreling. Don't be a fool! Quarreling doesn't happen on its own. We start it and feed it.

As charcoal to embers and as wood to fire, so is a quarrelsome man for kindling strife. Proverbs 26:21

We can stop! Are we willing to pay the price? If we claim to be followers of our Lord Jesus Christ—if he is truly Lord of our lives, then we will work to avoid quarrels and to be kind, able to teach without causing a quarrel and not resentful of others, which drives a quarrel.

Don't have anything to do with foolish and stupid arguments, because you know they produce quarrels. And the Lord's servant

must not quarrel; instead, he must be kind to everyone, able to teach, not resentful. 2 Timothy 2:23-24

It requires wisdom and obedience to avoid quarreling. Avoidance is godly. Pray for wisdom and the strength to obey. Become a peaceful peacemaker who can teach and express himself without inciting a conflict. If the hearts are right, we will succeed. Peacemakers must be humble and wise.

Reflection questions

How often do you find yourself in an argument?

How do you feel when you are wrong, or being told that you are wrong?

How well do you listen versus talk?

Do you turn others off with your words?

Do you "have to be" right?

Do you, or can you, walk away or keep quiet in order to avoid division and conflict?

Chapter Thirteen

Knowing Our Hearts

(Cutting out the deep roots of anger.)

Chapter Twelve was the last lesson that directly deals with anger. Hopefully the roots of your anger have been greatly healed. For most of us, dealing with our anger is a life-long process. This chapter and Chapter Fourteen will give a basis for continuation in your struggle against sinful anger.

If you think about what has happened in this course, it has mostly allowed you to see what goes on inside yourself. It has revealed hidden motives and drives within you. It has revealed hurts, wounds and scars in your heart. It has been an opening for the love and light of Christ to reveal those dark places of our hearts that need restoration and healing. This chapter will give you a set of disciplines to continue down this enlightening road. God is not finished with us yet. The completion of his work in us comes when Jesus returns to us or we return to him at death. But throughout this life we will be a continual work in progress. When Jesus returns, we will become like him in an instant as we see him in his completeness.

Dear friends, now we are children of God, and what we will be has not yet been made known. But we know that **when he appears, we shall be like him, for we shall see him as he is.** 1 John 3:2

The objective is to become like Jesus. As we see Jesus, we see the true state of our hearts. But a miraculous thing happens. When we see the truth, we change. Jesus is the truth—the truth about all things.

Anger can have deep roots. The solution is to discover and cut it out at the roots. This happens as we truly see Jesus.

Jesus also said that he is life. His Spirit living within us is a fountain of life. Jesus said that he is the light of life.

"I am the light of the world. Whoever follows me will never walk in darkness, but will have the **light of life."** John 8:12

For with you is the fountain of life; in your light we see light. Psalm 36:9

Jesus is the light of this dark world. Without him we grope around, lost in confusion and destruction. He is our only hope! We get lost in darkness. We may seek a direction, but without light, we usually get farther into a dark jungle. We normally think of this dark jungle as being outside of ourselves. But in reality, the dark jungle begins in our own hearts. If we truly understand ourselves, the outside will also be full of light. Jesus talked about being dark on the inside.

Your eye is the lamp of your body. When your eyes are good, your whole body also is full of light. But when they are bad, your body also is full of darkness. **See to it, then, that the light within you is not darkness.** Therefore, if your whole body is full of light, and no part of it dark, it will be completely lighted, as when the light of a lamp shines on you." Luke 11:34-36

If we want light in our life, we need to acquire light on the inside first. Jesus is that light that lives on our inside by his Spirit within us.

The man who walks in the dark does not know where he is going. Put your trust in the light while you have it, so that you may become sons of light." John 12:35-36

Our hearts deceive us, but the Lord is bigger than our hearts, and he reveals all truth—without deception.

The heart is deceitful above all things and beyond cure. Who can understand it? "I the LORD search the heart and examine the mind, to reward a man according to his conduct, according to what his deeds deserve." Jeremiah 17:9-10

He will bring to light what is hidden in darkness and will expose the motives of men's hearts. 1 Corinthians 4:5

We live with ourselves each and every day, yet few of us know ourselves. We can see our thoughts, our emotions and our actions, but do we know our hearts? Do we truly know why we feel and act the way that we do? The roots of anger are in the heart. We need to see our hearts to know the source of our anger.

The good man brings good things out of the good stored up in his heart, and the evil man brings evil things out of the evil stored up in his heart. For out of the overflow of his heart his mouth speaks. Luke 6:45

Jesus came so that our hearts would be filled with light to expose the hidden roots, to truly know ourselves. Jesus is this light. Jesus is the Word of God, which reveals our hearts. (John 1:1-14)

At this point it should be obvious that walking in the light is essential for a relationship with our Lord, and for any expectation to be delivered from anger or any other vice. So how do we walk in the light? There are several disciplines that should be a part of every Christian's structured life so that he remains in the light of Christ.

FIVE DISCIPLINES FOR WALKING IN THE LIGHT

❖   <u>**Study of his Word is seeking the light.**</u>

> For the word of God is living and active. Sharper than any double-edged sword, it penetrates even to dividing soul and spirit, joints and marrow; it judges the thoughts and attitudes of the heart. Nothing in all creation is hidden from God's sight. Everything is uncovered and laid bare before the eyes of him to whom we must give account.
> Hebrews 4:12-13

HOW TO STUDY   Have a time, place, duration and recorded plan. Be accountable.

1. Decide on a definite time to study each day, such as getting up early and studying before the work of the day begins. If you are a night person, it might be after everyone else has settled down for the evening, just before going to bed.
2. Commit to a time period, such as ten minutes per day. You can read longer, but tomorrow your commitment is the same—ten minutes. Make it a period you can commit to each and every day without missing. If ten minutes is too long, make it less. Do not increase

the time until you have demonstrated that you can maintain your commitment for at least two months.

3. Have a regular place to study. It may be sitting up in bed, a private room, the dinner table. The key is to make this a private discipline. It should not be random!

4. Keep track of your reading. If you are starting out, I recommend a one page spread sheet with each day of the year on it. Record each day where you read.

5. Be accountable to one or two others as to your recorded commitment.

6. If you should miss, get right back on schedule the next day.

DAY	JAN	FEB	MAR	APRIL	MAY	JUNE	JULY	AUG	SEPT	OCT	NOV	DEC
1												
2												
3												
4												
5												
6												
7												
8												
9												
10												
11												
12												
13												
14												
15												
16												
17												
18												
19												
20												
21												
22												
23												
24												
25												
26												
27												
28												
29												
30												
31												

❖ **Jesus is the Word; Jesus is the light. Be filled with the Spirit of Christ.**

Jesus came into this dark world as a light for mankind. This darkness resides in the hearts and minds of men. Our heavenly Father loves us. We are his creation, created for his purposes. He desires for us to have his light within us. We have already talked about renewing our minds through his written word. But we also need his Holy Spirit living within us to shine light on his word, upon the dark world around us and upon our darkened hearts. We are commanded from his Word to be filled with his Spirit.

Do not get drunk on wine, which leads to debauchery. Instead, **be filled with the Spirit**. Ephesians 5:18

Not only can we not see ourselves and the truth of the world around us without his light, we cannot see God without the light of his Holy Spirit within us.

For God, who said, "Let light shine out of darkness," **made his light shine in our hearts to give us the light of the knowledge of the glory of God in the face of Christ**. 2 Corinthians 4:6

How do we receive his Spirit? First we must hear about his Spirit and believe. Many received his Spirit immediately after being baptized. God desires to give us his Spirit. If we have not received his Spirit, we should ask. It is our responsibility to be filled. Jesus implores us to be filled with his light.

See to it, then, that the light within you is not darkness. Luke 11:35

God is not a selfish Father; he is lovingly waiting for our request to be filled with his Spirit.

If you then, though you are evil, know how to give good gifts to your children, **how much more will your Father in heaven give the Holy Spirit to those who ask him!**" Luke 11:13

Jesus does not want us to walk in darkness. He desires for all of us to be filled with his Word and his Spirit and in so doing, receive the light of life.

When Jesus spoke again to the people, he said, "I am the light of the world. Whoever follows me will never walk in darkness, but will have the light of life." John 8:12

❖ Confess to one another.

Walking in darkness is hiding the truth about our inner man. There is a saying: "Confession is good for the soul." Confession is the act of coming out of hiding about who we truly are inside. <u>Walking in the light is not being perfect; it is being truthful.</u> This is fundamental to having a real relationship with God and with one another.

Therefore **confess your sins to each other and pray for each other so that you may be healed.** The prayer of a righteous man is powerful and effective. James 5:16

We are forgiven when we confess our sins to God, but we can still separate ourselves from fellow Christians by hiding ourselves. Adam and Eve hid from God and covered themselves up to hide from each other. Before that they were in true fellowship with each other and with God. Hiding and division are the devil's objectives for you. He does not want for you to have true fellowship with God or man.

This is the message we have heard from him and declare to you: God is light; in him there is no darkness at all. If we claim to have fellowship with him yet walk in the darkness, we lie and do not live by the truth. But if we walk in the light, as he is in the light, we have fellowship with one another, and the blood of Jesus, his Son, purifies us from all sin.

If we claim to be without sin, we deceive ourselves and the truth is not in us. **If we confess our sins**, he is faithful and just and will forgive us our sins and purify us from all unrighteousness. **If we claim we have not sinned, we make him out to be a liar and his word has no place in our lives**. 1 John 1:5-10

How do we make this happen on a disciplined basis? We all need each other. We need close relationships with a few individuals where there are bonds of love and trust. It is in these close spiritual relationships that we can confess our sins, failures, struggles and shortcomings, as well as our victories, successes, strengths and blessings. Join a small, intimate, accountability group. Form a group of three to five of the same gender. Ask each other to report on the disciplines of this chapter. Share the things mentioned in this paragraph. Share what God is doing in your lives. Pray for one another. And use this time to reveal the things that go on deep inside of you. Bring them out into the light so that you may have true fellowship with your brothers or sisters in Christ and with God. Remember that Jesus promised that whenever two or three of you gather together for his name sake that he would be there in your midst. (Matthew 18:20) He will speak to you through one another. And you will leave enlightened about yourself and God. Is that not what has happened in the fellowship of this course?

❖ **Forgive and restore relationships—love.**

Anger destroys ourselves and it destroys our relationships with others. Bitterness and hatred toward others is a sign of unresolved problems due to walking in darkness. We are commanded to forgive and to get rid of all bitterness. Holding on to bitterness is a conscious act of remaining in darkness where healing does not occur. Unforgiveness is an act of our will, and it is a choice to walk in darkness.

Anyone who claims to be in the light but hates his brother is still in the darkness. Whoever loves his brother lives in the light, and there is nothing in him to make him stumble. But whoever hates his brother is in the darkness and walks around in the darkness; he does not know where he is going, because the darkness has blinded him. 1 John 2:9-11

Forgiveness may be difficult, even sacrificial, but it is a choice on our part. The greatest harm is not to the offending party, but to ourselves. When we choose not to forgive, we have chosen to be separated from God. We have chosen to be blind and lost in darkness. We have chosen to stumble and fall. If we want to be free from destructive bondage, whether it is anger or many other bondages, such as depression, anxiety, addictions, sexual, etc., then we need to consciously walk in forgiveness.

❖ **Repent and come out of darkness.**

Jesus came that we would have his abundant life (John 10:10). This abundant life comes by coming out of darkness into his light. Repentance is turning from the ways of darkness and walking in the ways of Jesus, the light. Repentance is a prerequisite for salvation, but repentance is not a one-time act. We must choose to walk in the light daily. Notice in the following description of Jesus that remaining in darkness or coming out into the light is a deliberate choice on our part.

This is the verdict: Light has come into the world, but **men loved darkness instead** of light because their deeds were evil. Everyone who does evil hates the light, and will not come into the light for fear that his deeds will be exposed. But whoever lives by the truth comes into the light, so that it may be seen plainly that what he has done has been done through God." John 3:19-21

Repentance is our choice to turn the direction of our lives from the easy, wide road that leads to death onto the harder, narrower road that leads to life. This is a daily choice. We are all on this road at some place.

Enter through the narrow gate. For wide is the gate and **broad is the road that leads to destruction**, and many enter through it. But small is the gate and **narrow the road that leads to life**, and only a few find it. Matthew 7:13-14

We will not reach either end of this road until Jesus returns. For now, the concern is not as much where we are on this road, for we are all at different levels of maturity. The real question is which direction have we chosen to travel? Repentance is the choice of our direction. This is a daily choice, to strive for the light of life or to just roll downhill into darkness and destruction. If we have chosen to seek life, we will be making steady progress toward becoming like Christ. This is an act of our will, with a transformation through the Word of God, empowered and instructed by the Holy Spirit and paid for by the blood of Jesus.

In conclusion, we may hide our hearts; thinking we have deceived man and God, but God already knows everything that goes on within us, so why not trust him with it now. Today we are forgiven for the things we bring into the light, and the Holy Spirit will cleanse us from within because of the blood of Jesus. And if we do not bring things out into the light now, they all will be brought out of hiding in the end. So be wise and start now so that healing can occur.

Therefore judge nothing before the appointed time; wait till the Lord comes. He will bring to light what is hidden in darkness and will expose the motives of men's hearts. At that time each will receive his praise from God. 1 Corinthians 4:5 (Proverbs 26:24-26)

We are commanded to flee the deeds of darkness and to expose their deceptive ploys. Let's begin by allowing the light of Christ to expose the hidden places within our own hearts. This is the secret to true freedom within and deliverance from anger or anything else that holds us captive.

Have nothing to do with the fruitless deeds of darkness, but rather **expose them**. Ephesians 5:11

Reflection questions

How well do you think you know your true motives? (Why do you swear, smoke, drink, overeat, take drugs, brag, argue, compete, achieve, get angry, depressed or anxious? Etc.)

Have you asked God to fill you with his Holy Spirit?

Do you have a few close friends that you can trust with your true feelings—good or bad?

Do you confess your faults with your close friends?

What are your Bible study and prayer habits?

What has God revealed to you about yourself through this study?

Chapter Fourteen

Knowing God's Love

As we began this course, we talked about being created in the image of God. We were created to be like God in nature. Because of Adam's sin, we have all acquired a sinful nature from birth. Our struggle in this life is to rid ourselves of our sinful nature and to live according to the nature of God. That is why, through Jesus, God sent his Holy Spirit to live within man. It is so we might have the power and nature of God living within us.

But is that all there is to it, just having the Spirit reside within us? This life of God, this eternal life that only God has, is acquired by knowing God. Jesus said,

> Now **this is eternal life: that they may know you,** the only true God, and Jesus Christ, whom you have sent. John 17:3

So how do we come to know God? We also read,

Dear friends, let us love one another, for **love comes from God. Everyone who loves has been born of God and knows God. Whoever does not love does not know God, because God is love.** 1 John 4:7-8

And so we know and rely on the love God has for us. **God is love. Whoever lives in love lives in God, and God in him.** 1 John 4:16

In our anger, in our addictions, in our broken relationships, in our unforgiveness, in our selfishness, etc.; in all of our sinful nature we are producing spiritual death, and most of us can testify to the struggles of death within our spirits. However, when we live a life of love we are living as God lives, for God is love. This is the secret for passing from death to life.

We know that we have passed from death to life, because we love our brothers. Anyone who does not love remains in death. 1 John 3:14

What is love? Love may have good feelings, but love is not feelings. In fact, if we are pursuing the good feelings, it is not love. Love is sacrificial. Jesus said that the greatest love is to give up our life for another. (John 15:13) That is what he did for us; he gave up his life so that we could have his life—true life that comes by his Spirit. Jesus told us to love even our enemies (Matthew 5:38-48). To love someone is to live for their good. If we are in the relationship for what we get from it, it is not love. Love is not self-serving; it is serving others. If we are rewarded with good feelings, thanks be to God, but we do not love for what we receive.

God is love. If we thoroughly knew his love, all of our problems, all of our sin, all of our cares and burdens would flee. Knowing God's love is key to becoming like God in his love.

Defeating anger is a spiritual battle. Knowing God's love for us is critical to victory.

Knowing God's love comes from two directions:

One, we experience God's direct love for us. We see him blessing us in the circumstances of our lives. Thankfulness is the heart-felt recognition of specific ways in which God has poured out his loving blessings upon us. Knowing God's almighty hand in our lives is to know his love. We have already talked about being thankful as the antidote for grumbling and complaining.

Two, we come to know God's love when he loves others through us. This is the most powerful. "God is love." 1 John 4:7-21 God lives within the Christian by his Holy Spirit.

God has poured out his love into our hearts by the Holy Spirit, whom he has given us. Romans 5:5

When we love one another, we experience God's love flowing through us. It flows back and forth within his people. When we experience his flow of love to others and we open ourselves up to love, we will see his love from our hearts in a way that is beyond intellectual description. Look closely at Paul's instruction to the people of the Church of Ephesus.

For this reason I kneel before the Father, from whom his whole family in heaven and on earth derives its name. I pray that out of his glorious riches he may strengthen you with **power** through his Spirit in your inner being, so that Christ may dwell in your hearts through faith. And I pray that **you, being rooted and established in love**, may have **power**, together with all the saints, to grasp how wide and long and high and deep is the love of Christ, and **to know this love that surpasses knowledge—that you may be filled to the measure of all the fullness of God**. Ephesians 3:14-19

Notice that he says when we love that we will have power to grasp the fullness of Christ's love, and that this understanding goes beyond just knowledge. He proclaims another incredible fact. When we are rooted and established in love we will be filled with the fullness of God. We will be so filled with God that there will be complete healing of wounds of rejection or hurt of any kind from others. **And our anger will have lost its fuse.**

The product of our faith in God and the Lord Jesus Christ is that we express love to others.

The only thing that counts is faith expressing itself through love. Galatians 5:6

God created us for his love to flow through us to others. We selfishly hold onto what is ours, afraid that we may not have enough for ourselves. But God is our resource who has no limitations. He desires to provide for those who freely give of his wealth so that they can keep on giving. (2 Corinthians 9:8-11) We are to pour out his love even on our enemies. God will love us in the same measure we use to love others—and we will see his love flowing through us. (Luke 6:27-38)

As Paul wrote, knowing this love goes beyond knowledge. It only comes by standing in the flow of his love through us. Begin by loving others. His love through us is the power of God. It is the fullness of God. <u>**When you know how much God loves you and how much he loves others, your anger will not be an issue.**</u>

Remember that Christianity is a relationship with God and others based on love. Jesus summed up the entire Law and the Prophets with these two commands:

Jesus replied: "'Love the Lord your God with all your heart and with all your soul and with all your mind.' This is the first and greatest commandment. And the second is like it: 'Love your neighbor as

146

yourself.' All the Law and the Prophets hang on these two commandments." Matthew 22:37-40 (also read 1 John 2:9-11, 3:11-24)

Loving one another is the essence of walking with God. Christianity is deliberate. Love is deliberate. We love out of obedience to Jesus, but the blessings are immeasurable. In fact, when we love, we find the treasure that we are all searching for, the only one that heals all and fully satisfies.

Reflection questions

What are the greatest needs of those around you? (beyond physical needs or desires)

How can you meet their needs?

What plans could you make to get started at meeting their needs?

God loves you! May he bless your heart with the understanding of his infinite love for you. May you find life in Him through Jesus Christ. May you be free inside. And may you love others with the love God has provided by his Holy Spirit living within you to give you his life. He loves you; walk in his love. May his love flow through you, not your anger.

Made in the USA
Middletown, DE
23 February 2019